THE POCKET
UNIVERSAL
PRINCIPLES
OF DESIGN

NUDGE
HIERARCHY
KISS
CONSISTENCY
ANTHROPOMORPHISM
FIGURE-GROUND
DEVELOPMENT CYCLE
STORYTELLING
FRAMING
COMMON FATE
CLOSURE
ACCESSIBILITY
CONTROL
YELLOW EFFECTS
CROWD INTELLIGENCE
PRIMING
FEEDBACK LOOP
FEATURE CREEP
FORGIVENESS
MAYA
SIMILARITY
MODULARITY
MAPPING
FITTS' LAW
SCARCITY
FIBONACCI SEQUENCE
DESIGN BY COMMITTEE
ROOT CAUSE
ABBE
ENTRY POINT
REDUNDANCY
COMPARISON
CONSTRAINT
SOCIAL TRAP
FACE-ISM RATIO
SATISFICING
80/20 RULE
CONFIRMATION
PROSPECT-REFUGE
INATTENTIONAL BLINDNESS
WABI-SABI
STICKINESS
VEBLEN EFFECT
FEEDBACK LOOP
SHAPING
LEFT-DIGIT EFFECT
FLOW
BLUE EFFECTS
WEAKEST LINK
HORROR VACUI
VISIBILITY
AFFORDANCE
DESIRE LINE
HIGHLIGHTING
ERRORS

THE POCKET
UNIVERSAL PRINCIPLES OF DESIGN

William Lidwell   Kritina Holden   Jill Butler

ROCKPORT

Brimming with creative inspiration, how-to projects, and useful information to enrich your everyday life, Quarto Knows is a favorite destination for those pursuing their interests and passions. Visit our site and dig deeper with our books into your area of interest: Quarto Creates, Quarto Cooks, Quarto Homes, Quarto Lives, Quarto Drives, Quarto Explores, Quarto Gifts, or Quarto Kids.

© 2015 by Rockport Publishers, Inc.
This edition published in 2015

First published in 2015 by Rockport Publishers,
an imprint of The Quarto Group,
100 Cummings Center, Suite 265-D,
Beverly, MA 01915, USA.
T (978) 282-9590 F (978) 283-2742
www.QuartoKnows.com

Rockport Publishers titles are also available at discount for retail, wholesale, promotional, and bulk purchase. For details, contact the Special Sales Manager by email at specialsales@quarto.com or by mail at The Quarto Group, Attn: Special Sales Manager, 401 Second Avenue North, Suite 310, Minneapolis, MN 55401, USA.

Library of Congress Cataloging-in-Publication Data Available
ISBN: 978-1-63159-040-5
10 9

Design: Stuff Creators Design

Printed in China

FOR FRIEND AND MENTOR

David B. Palumbo

Contents

Author Favorites
Our Most Used Principles of Design

Less and More.
Dieter Rams

3D Projection

A tendency to see things as three-dimensional when certain visual cues are present.

- People see two-dimensional things as three-dimensional when certain visual cues are present.

- When items are relatively larger, lower, less dense in pattern, lighter, clearer, or in front of other objects, they are perceived to be closer.

- When items are relatively smaller, higher, denser in pattern, bluer, blurrier, or behind other objects, they are perceived to be farther away.

- Consider 3D projection in the depiction of three-dimensional elements and environments. Strongest depth effects are achieved when the visual cues are used in combination; therefore, use as many of the cues as possible to achieve the strongest effect.

See Also   Common Fate • Figure-Ground • Law of Prägnanz
Top-Down Lighting Bias • Visuospatial Resonance

Applying 3D projection in sidewalk art can create stunning three-dimensional effects on two-dimensional surfaces.

80/20 Rule

A high percentage of effects in any large system is caused by a low percentage of variables.

- Proposed by the economist Vilfredo Pareto, who observed that 20 percent of the Italian people possessed 80 percent of the wealth.

- Applying the 80/20 rule means identifying and focusing resources on the critical 20 percent. Focusing on aspects of a design beyond the critical 20 percent yields diminishing returns.

- For example, 80 percent of a product's usage involves 20 percent of its features; 80 percent of a product's bugs are caused by 20 percent of its components.

- Use the 80/20 rule to assess the relative value of elements, target areas of redesign and optimization, and focus resources in an efficient manner. Note that 80/20 is just an estimate. The actual percentages can be more or less (e.g., 70/30, 90/10).

See Also   Cost-Benefit • Feature Creep • Hanlon's Razor
Normal Distribution • Ockham's Razor

In 1979, most believed that a music player with no radio, no speakers, no recording function, and small headphones was doomed to fail. Sony proved them wrong. The Walkman possessed the critical 20 percent of what people wanted—portability and tape playback—enabling the rest to be cut.

Abbe

Measure things as close to their action as possible.

- Proposed by the German physicist Ernst Abbe.

- Abbe errors are angular errors that increase with distance. For example, wobble from a bent axle increases with the length of the axle. The Abbe principle prevents this type of error.

- The Abbe principle states that the best measurements are achieved when taken as close to the action as possible. For example, placing a temperature sensor near a heat source will result in more accurate measurements than a sensor placed farther away.

- The principle also has implications for the design of mechanisms. Actuators and bearings should be placed as close to lines of action as possible.

- Consider the Abbe principle in measurement, and the design of mechanical systems and structures. Locate measurement devices and components as close to the areas of action as possible.

See Also   Error • Redundancy • Saint-Venant's Principle

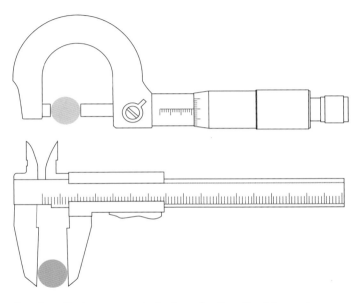

A caliper that measures in its line of action (top) is more accurate than a caliper that measures away from its line of action (bottom).

004 **Accessibility**

Things should be designed to be usable, without modification, by as many people as possible.

- Historically, accessibility in design focused on accommodating people with disabilities.

- Modern practice accepts that most accommodations can be designed to benefit everyone.

- Make things perceptible by everyone. For example, position controls and information so that seated and standing people can perceive them.

- Make things usable by everyone. For example, minimize repetitive actions and the need for sustained physical effort.

- Make things learnable by everyone. For example, use redundant coding methods (e.g., textual, iconic, and tactile) on controls and signage.

- Make the consequences of errors non-catastrophic, and reversible whenever possible.

See Also Affordance • Forgiveness • Normal Distribution

Inventor Dean Kamen demonstrating the iBot, a Transformer-like wheelchair that makes a world designed for those who can stand and walk accessible to wheelchair users.

Aesthetic-Usability Effect

Aesthetic things are perceived to be easier to use than ugly things.

- Aesthetic things are often subjectively rated as easier to use, even when no usability advantage can be objectively measured.

- Aesthetic things are more effective at fostering positive attitudes than ugly things, making people more tolerant when problems are encountered.

- Aesthetic things are more likely to be tried, accepted, displayed, and repeatedly used than ugly things.

- Aspire to create aesthetically pleasing designs. It is more than ornamentation—it is an investment in user acceptance, forgiveness, and satisfaction.

See Also   Attractiveness Bias • Cognitive Dissonance
Form Follows Function • IKEA Effect

People display the HomeHero extinguisher on counters due to its striking aesthetic, making it more accessible in emergencies.

Affordance

The physical characteristics of a thing influence its function and use.

- The form of a thing makes it better suited for some functions than others. For example, wheels afford rolling, and negatively afford being stationary.

- The form of a thing makes it better suited for some interactions than others. For example, buttons afford pushing, and negatively afford pulling.

- When affordances are good, things perform efficiently and are intuitive to use. When affordances are bad, things perform poorly and are hard to use.

- Design things to afford proper use, and to negatively afford improper use. When affordances are correctly applied, it will seem inconceivable that a thing can function or be used otherwise.

See Also   Constraint • Desire Line • Mapping • Nudge

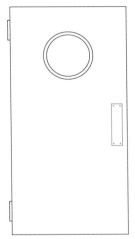

The push action required to open the left door conflicts with the "pull" affordance of the handle. The sign is a poor fix because it will usually be read after people pull the handle. By replacing the handle with a flat plate, the conflict is eliminated and the sign becomes unnecessary. The "push" affordance of the plate eliminates the possibility of error or confusion.

Alignment

The placement of elements such that edges line up along common rows or columns, or their bodies along a common center.

- Alignment among elements in a design creates a sense of unity and cohesion.

- Left- and right-aligned text blocks provide better alignment cues than center-aligned text blocks.

- Justified text provides more alignment cues than unjustified text, and should be used in complex compositions with many elements.

- Treat the edges of the design medium (e.g., edge of a page) and the natural positions on the medium (e.g., centerlines) as alignment elements.

- Align every element in your designs with one or more other elements. This will improve the design's perceived stability and overall aesthetic.

See Also   Area Alignment • Mapping • Signal-to-Noise Ratio

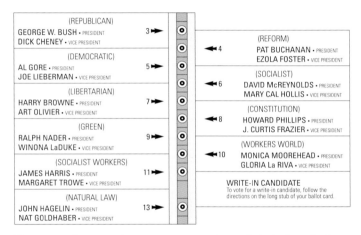

The poor alignment between rows and punch-hole lines in the infamous Palm Beach County butterfly ballot led to errors that awarded Pat Buchanan votes intended for Al Gore, costing Gore the U.S. presidential election of 2000.

Anthropomorphism

A preference for things that appear humanlike or exhibit humanlike characteristics.

- People tend to ascribe humanlike characteristics to things that look or act like humans. This results in a preference for anthropomorphic forms.

- Anthropomorphic forms are evaluated more emotionally, and are less sensitive to negative information in buying decisions. Non-anthropomorphic forms are evaluated more analytically.

- Use contoured or hourglass proportions to elicit feminine and sexual associations. Use round forms to elicit babylike associations. Use angular forms to elicit masculine and aggressive associations.

- Consider anthropomorphic forms to attract attention and establish emotional connections.

See Also   Baby-Face Bias • Supernormal Stimulus
Uncanny Valley • Waist-to-Hip Ratio

1899   1900   1915   1991   2007

Coca-Cola bottles have evolved over the last 100 years, but the more anthropomorphic bottles continue to stand out in terms of their unique aesthetic and emotional appeal.

Apparent Motion

An illusion of motion created when images are displayed in rapid succession.

- Apparent motion occurs when still images are presented in rapid succession at different positions and orientations, creating the illusion of motion.

- Apparent motion can be created by changing the position or orientation of objects across images, or by moving background elements around a fixed object.

- The rate of image presentation can be as low as 10 images or frames per second. The standard frame rate for television and movies is 24–30 frames per second. Frame rates of 60+ frames per second are indistinguishable from reality.

- Consider apparent motion when creating animations or videos. Maximize frame rates to present the most natural motion possible.

See Also 3D Projection • Common Fate • Figure-Ground Inattentional Blindness • Visuospatial Resonance

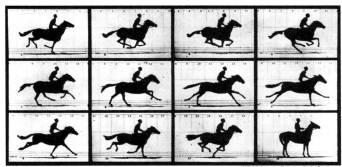

THE HORSE IN MOTION.

Illustrated by
MUYBRIDGE

"SALLIE GARDNER," owned by LELAND STANFORD; running at a 1.40 gait over the Palo Alto track, 19th June, 1878.

A motion study by Eadweard Muybridge. When the images are displayed in rapid succession, the illusion of motion is created. Experience the effect by flipping the top-right page corners.

Archetypes

Universal patterns of form, social role, and story that have innate appeal.

- People are instinctively drawn to certain patterns. Such patterns are often referred to as archetypes.

- Interest in archetypal patterns provided our early human ancestors with an adaptive advantage. Modern humans have inherited this interest.

- Archetypal forms include faces, horns and canine teeth, snakes, spiders, and sexual forms.

- Archetypal social roles include the hero, rebel, mentor, trickster, and villain.

- Archetypal stories include the quest, tragedy, voyage and return, and conquering the monster.

- Consider appropriate archetypes in your designs to capture and hold attention.

See Also Affordance • Black Effects • Contour Bias
Mimicry • Supernormal Stimulus • Threat Detection

Explorations of archetypal forms as a way to tell people 10,000 years from now to "stay away" from a nuclear waste repository.

Area Alignment

Alignment based on the area of elements versus the edges of elements.

- Asymmetrical elements often do not align properly using conventional edge- or center-based methods.

- In such cases, align elements based on their areas or visual weights, not based on their edges or rectangular centers.

- This technique must be applied using the designer's eye and judgment, balancing elements on the axis of alignment as if they had mass.

- The principle applies to ragged-edge text blocks as well as graphical elements.

- Align based on area when elements are nonuniform and asymmetrical.

See Also Alignment • Closure • Good Continuation
Orientation Sensitivity • Uniform Connectedness

The left column is center-aligned using the rectangular centers of figures. The right column is center-aligned using the areas of figures. Note the improvement achieved by area alignment.

Attractiveness Bias

A tendency to view attractive people as intelligent, competent, moral, and sociable.

- Attractive people are perceived to possess positive intellectual and social attributes.

- Attributes of attractiveness include symmetrical facial features, clear skin, ideal waist-hip-ratios, indications of status, and signs of health and fertility.

- Women enhance their attractiveness to men by exaggerating fertility (e.g., lipstick for red lips).

- Men enhance their attractiveness to women by exaggerating status (e.g., expensive cars).

- Consider the attractiveness bias in contexts involving human interaction and images of people, such as sales and advertising.

See Also Baby-Face Bias • Face-ism Ratio • Gloss Bias
Red Effects • Waist-to-Hip Ratio

Most radio listeners of the first Kennedy-Nixon debate believed Nixon won. Most television viewers believed Kennedy won.

Baby-Face Bias

A tendency to see things with baby-faced features as having the personality characteristics of babies.

- People and things with round features, large eyes, small noses, high foreheads, short chins, and light hair and skin are perceived to be more naïve, helpless, and honest than those with mature features.

- Large round heads and eyes appear to be the strongest facial cues contributing to the bias.

- The bias applies to all anthropomorphic things, including people, animals, and cartoon characters, and products such as bottles, appliances, and vehicles.

- Consider the baby-face bias in the design of characters or products when facelike features are prominent. In advertising, use mature-faced people when conveying expertise and authority; use baby-faced people when conveying innocence and honesty.

See Also Anthropomorphism • Contour Bias • Face-ism Ratio
Mimicry • Savanna Preference

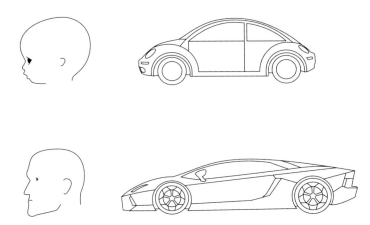

Round products tend to elicit baby-face associations. Angular products tend to elicit mature and masculine associations.

Back-of-the-Dresser

All parts of a design should be held to the same standard of quality.

- Proposed informally by Steve Jobs, American entrepreneur and personal computer pioneer.

- The principle asserts that the craftsmanship applied by designers and developers to areas not ordinarily visible to customers is a good indicator of product quality—it is proof whether they applied consistent craftsmanship to all aspects of the product.

- Indications of craftsmanship include quality materials, precision fit, uniformity of finish, internal consistency, and maker marks or signatures. These elements reflect the passion and care (or lack thereof) of the creators.

- Apply excellent design and development to all aspects of products. Treat invisible areas as if they were visible, and include them in testing and evaluation. Light is the best disinfectant for shoddy craftsmanship.

See Also   Aesthetic-Usability Effect • Consistency
Feature Creep • Form Follows Function • Framing

Brick fronts and HardiePlank backs lower costs, but raise suspicions about what other out-of-sight corners were cut.

Biophilia Effect

A state of reduced stress and improved concentration resulting from nature views.

- Exposure to natural environments replete with lush green flora and visible water reduces stress and confers restorative cognitive and physical benefits.

- The effect is likely a vestigial response to ancestral habitats, related to the savanna preference.

- Imagery of nature depicted in art and photographs, as well as interior plants, can trigger the biophilia effect.

- The strength of the effect corresponds to the level of exposure. Office environments with one plant are unlikely to trigger the effect. Office environments with ample greenery are more likely to trigger the effect.

- Consider the biophilia effect in the design of all environments, but especially environments in which learning, healing, and concentration are paramount.

See Also Cathedral Effect • Green Effects • Prospect-Refuge
Savanna Preference • Self-Similarity

The High Line park of New York provides a beautiful biophilic retreat amidst the hustle and bustle of big city life.

Black Effects

A set of cognitive and behavioral effects triggered by exposure to the color black.

- Black is universally associated with evil and foreboding, likely due to an evolved association with darkness and vulnerability to nocturnal predators.

- Black signals aggression, dominance, and dirtiness.

- Sports teams wearing predominately black uniforms are perceived to be more aggressive and more likely to cheat than those wearing light colors. Accordingly, they incur more penalties.

- Black products are generally perceived to be classy, high value, and timeless.

- Use black to increase perceived value in products and perceived authority in people. Consider using black to signal aggression and intimidate adversaries.

See Also Archetypes • Red Effects • Supernormal Stimulus Threat Detection • White Effects

Black effects make black dogs less adoptable than lighter-colored dogs. Animal shelters call this "black dog syndrome".

Blue Effects

A set of cognitive and behavioral effects triggered by exposure to the color blue.

- Blue is the world's most popular color, and is commonly associated with water and purity—except in food contexts, where it is associated with spoilage.

- Blue signals friendliness and peacefulness (e.g., color of the United Nations).

- Blue fosters openness and creativity, and promotes aspirational thinking.

- Blue promotes alertness and well-being during the day, but can disrupt sleep at night.

- Use blue when you need a generally popular color, though avoid blue in food-related contexts. Consider blue to promote friendliness, open-mindedness, and aspirational thinking. Use blue lighting to increase alertness, but avoid it in sleep environments.

See Also Biophilia Effect • Gloss Bias • Green Effects
Prospect-Refuge • Savanna Preference

Blue works best for aspirational messages (e.g., white teeth).
Red works best for risk-avoidance (e.g., preventing cavities).

Cathedral Effect

High ceilings promote abstract thinking. Low ceilings promote detail-oriented thinking.

- Conspicuous ceiling height—that is, noticeably low or noticeably high ceilings—promotes different types of cognition, with high ceilings promoting abstract thinking and creativity, and low ceilings promoting concrete and detail-oriented thinking. No effect is observed if the ceiling height goes unnoticed.

- The effect may be due to priming, or a vestigial preference for high tree canopies and open skies, as would have been common on the African savannas.

- Favor large rooms with high ceilings for tasks requiring creativity and out-of-the-box thinking. Favor small rooms with low ceilings for tasks requiring detail-oriented work (e.g., surgical operating room). Favor high ceilings to extend the time in which visitors remain on site (e.g., casino) and low ceilings to minimize loitering (e.g., fast-food restaurant).

See Also   Priming • Prospect-Refuge • Savanna Preference

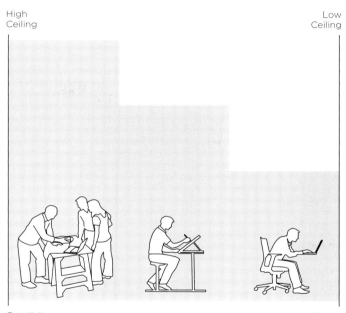

High
Ceiling

Low
Ceiling

Creativity

Focus

High ceilings promote abstract and creative thinking. Low
ceilings promote concrete and detail-oriented thinking.

Chunking

Grouping units of information to make them easier to process and remember.

- The term chunk refers to a unit of information in short-term memory—a word, or a series of numbers. Information that is chunked is easier to remember.

- For example, most people cannot remember a ten-digit number for more than 30 seconds. However, by breaking the number into three chunks (i.e., such as a phone number) recall performance is equivalent to recalling one 5-digit number.

- The original estimate of the maximum number of chunks that can be efficiently processed and recalled was 7±2. The modern estimate is 4±1 chunks.

- Chunk information when people are required to recall and retain information. In high-stress environments, chunk critical controls and information in anticipation of diminished cognitive performance.

See Also   Mnemonic Device • Performance Load
Recognition Over Recall • Signal-to-Noise Ratio

Principle Chunk

Description Chunk

Example Chunk

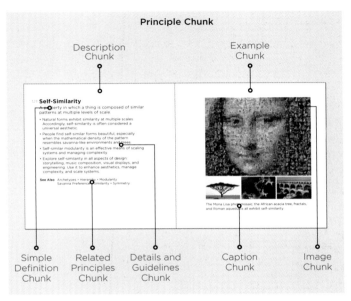

Self-Similarity

A property in which a thing is composed of similar patterns at multiple levels of scale

- Natural forms exhibit similarity at multiple scales Accordingly, self-similarity is often considered a universal aesthetic.
- People find self-similar forms beautiful, especially when the mathematical density of the pattern resembles savanna-like environments and trees.
- Self-similar modularity is an effective means of scaling systems and managing complexity
- Explore self-similarity in all aspects of design: storytelling, music composition, visual displays, and engineering Use it to enhance aesthetics, manage complexity, and scale systems.

See Also Archetypes • Hierarchy • Modularity Savanna Preference • Similarity • Symmetry

The Mona Lisa photo mosaic, the African acacia tree, fractals, and Roman aqueducts all exhibit self-similarity

Simple Definition Chunk

Related Principles Chunk

Details and Guidelines Chunk

Caption Chunk

Image Chunk

This book uses multiple levels of chunking to make design principles easier to read, understand, and remember.

020

Classical Conditioning

A method of influencing how people react to a particular thing by repeatedly presenting it with other things they either like or dislike.

- The influence occurs at an unconscious level, and results in a physical or emotional reaction.

- Classical conditioning is commonly employed in animal training, behavior modification, and advertising.

- For example, presenting images of attractive people with a product creates positive feelings for that product. Conversely, presenting disturbing images of extreme violence or injury with a product creates negative feelings for that product.

- The stronger the reaction to a thing, the easier it will be to generalize that reaction to other things.

- Use classical conditioning to influence emotional appeal. Pair designs with appropriate stimuli to promote positive or negative associations.

See Also Aesthetic-Usability Effect • Mere-Exposure Effect
Operant Conditioning • Shaping

This poster uses before and after images of a drunk driving victim to condition negative feelings about drunk driving.

021

Closure

A tendency to complete incomplete or interrupted forms and patterns.

- One of the Gestalt principles of perception.

- Patterns that require closure for completion grab attention and are considered more interesting.

- Closure likely evolved as a form of threat detection, enabling human ancestors to reflexively detect partially obscured threats, like snakes in the grass.

- Closure is strongest when patterns are simple and elements are located near one another.

- Use closure to reduce complexity and increase the interestingness of designs. When designs involve simple and recognizable patterns, consider removing areas to trigger closure in viewers.

See Also   Flow • Threat Detection • Zeigarnik Effect

Engaging people to complete or "close" logos is an effective means of grabbing and holding attention.

022

Cognitive Dissonance

A state of mental discomfort due to incompatible attitudes, thoughts, and beliefs.

- Cognitive dissonance is a state of mental stress due to conflicting thoughts or values. It also occurs when new information conflicts with existing thoughts or values.

- When a person is in a state of cognitive dissonance, they seek to make their incompatible thoughts or values compatible with one another.

- For example, diamond sellers urge consumers to demonstrate their love by buying diamonds, creating cognitive dissonance in consumers—i.e., dissonance between the love that they have for another, and the pressure to prove that love by buying diamonds.

- Consider cognitive dissonance in persuasion contexts. Alleviate cognitive dissonance by reducing the importance of conflicting thoughts, adding new confirmatory thoughts, or changing the conflicting thoughts to appear compatible.

See Also   Expectation Effects • Framing • Sunk Cost Effect

Benjamin Franklin was a formidable social engineer. He once asked a rival legislator to lend him a rare book, which he did. The rival greatly disliked Franklin, but had done him this favor. How to alleviate the conflict? The two became lifelong friends.

023

Common Fate

Things that move in similar directions are perceived to be related.

- One of the Gestalt principles of perception.

- Things that move together in common directions are perceived as a single unit or chunk, and are interpreted to be more related than things that move at different times or in different directions.

- Perceived relatedness is strongest when motion occurs at the same time, velocity, and direction. As these factors vary, perceived relatedness decreases.

- Common fate influences whether things are perceived as figures or ground: moving elements are perceived as figures, and stationary elements as ground.

- Consider common fate when displaying information with moving or flickering elements. Related elements should move at the same time, velocity, and direction, or flicker at the same time, frequency, and intensity.

See Also   Chunking • Figure-Ground • Good Continuation
Similarity • Uniform Connectedness

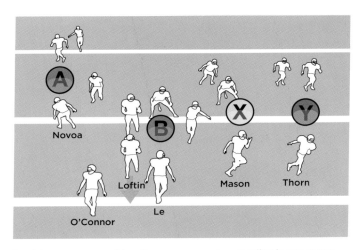

In video games, making the names and controller icons move with the players groups them, simplifying playability by making it clear who is being controlled and how to control them.

024

Comparison

A method of highlighting relationships by depicting information in controlled ways.

- One of the most compelling ways to present evidence is to compare things apples-to-apples, within one eyespan, and against familiar benchmarks.

- Comparing things apples-to-apples means comparing the same variables in the same way.

- Comparing things within one eyespan means presenting data side by side so that differences are easily detectable.

- Comparing things against benchmarks means providing context so that the significance of differences can be understood.

- Use comparisons to highlight relationships and present evidence. Ensure that the variables compared are apples-to-apples, presented within one eyespan, and contextualized with appropriate benchmarks.

See Also   Framing • Garbage In-Garbage Out • Layering
Signal-to-Noise Ratio • Visibility

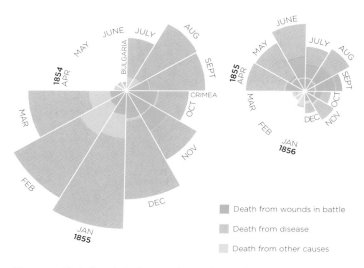

Diagram of the Causes of Mortality in the Army in the East

Death from wounds in battle

Death from disease

Death from other causes

Florence Nightingale's Coxcomb graph used comparison to make the case that the predominant threat to British troops was not the Russians, but cholera, dysentery, and typhus.

025

Confirmation

A technique for preventing errors by requiring verification before actions are performed.

- A technique used to verify critical actions, inputs, or commands. Confirmations provide a means for verifying that actions and inputs are intentional and correct before they are executed.

- There are two basic confirmation types: dialogs and two-step operations.

- Dialogs ask if an action was intended, indicate the consequences of the action, and then provide a means to either verify or cancel the action. Two-step operations involve a preliminary step that must occur prior to the actual action or input.

- Use confirmations to minimize errors. Avoid using too many confirmations, else they will be ignored. Allow noncritical confirmations to be disabled.

See Also Affordance • Constraint • Errors • Forgiveness
Garbage In-Garbage Out • Redundancy

This industrial paper-cutting machine requires a two-step confirmation: both hands must depress safety releases (ensuring that they are not in harm's way) before the foot press is unlocked to cut the paper.

026

Confirmation Bias

A tendency to favor information that confirms pre-existing views.

- The confirmation bias is a tendency to focus on information that supports pre-existing views, and to ignore information that contradicts pre-existing views.

- Effects of the bias include overconfidence, selective memory, poor decision making, and resistance to change in light of contrary evidence.

- For example, a person who believes the moon landing was faked seeks out information that confirms this belief, and ignores evidence to the contrary.

- The bias is strongest for beliefs in which there has been significant emotional investment.

- Consider the confirmation bias when conducting research and development. Recognition of the bias is the best antidote. Expose yourself to contrary opinions and independent critiques. Beware exploitation of the confirmation bias by those with political agendas.

See Also   Cognitive Dissonance • Selection Bias

Global Surface Temperature

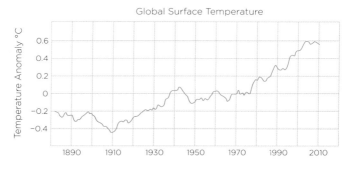

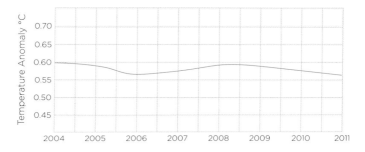

The long-term trend clearly indicates rising global temperatures, which is why denialists tend to focus on the short-term trend.

027

Consistency

Usability and learnability improve when similar things have similar meanings and functions.

- Consistency enables people to efficiently transfer knowledge to new contexts, learn new things quickly, and focus attention on the relevant aspects of a task.

- Make things aesthetically consistent to enhance recognition and communicate membership.

- Make things functionally consistent to leverage existing knowledge about functionality and use.

- Make things internally consistent to improve usability, and to signal that a thing has been well designed and not cobbled together.

- Make things externally consistent to extend the benefits of internal consistency to other things.

- Use consistency in all aspects of design. When design standards exist, generally follow them—but remember: "A foolish consistency is the hobgoblin of little minds."

See Also Back-of-the-Dresser • Feature Creep • Mimicry
Recognition Over Recall • Similarity

Consistency enables international travelers to understand
traffic signs even when they don't speak the local language.

028

Constancy

A tendency to perceive objects as unchanging
despite visual cues to the contrary.

- People tend to perceive familiar objects as constant
  and unchanging, despite changes in perspective,
  lighting, color, or size.

- This indicates that perception involves more than
  simply receiving sensory inputs; rather, it is a process
  of continuously reconciling sensory inputs with
  memories about the properties of things in the world.

- For example, people viewed at a distance look smaller
  than the same people viewed up close, but the
  perception of their size is constant. Other types of
  constancy include brightness, shape, and loudness.

- Consider constancy when presenting information in
  atypical contexts, such as 3D images on 2D displays.
  Use recognizable objects and distance cues to provide
  size and shape references for unfamiliar objects.

See Also 3D Projection • Comparison • Rosetta Stone

The penny in this picture appears oversized, but we know its size is constant, making it a useful size reference for the frog.

029

Constraint

Limiting the actions that can be performed to
simplify use and prevent error.

- There are two types of constraints: physical
  and psychological.

- Physical constraints limit the range of possible actions
  by redirecting physical motion. The three kinds of
  physical constraints are paths, axes, and barriers.

- Psychological constraints limit the range of possible
  actions by leveraging the way people perceive and
  think. The three kinds of psychological constraints are
  symbols, conventions, and mappings.

- Use constraints to minimize errors. Use physical
  constraints to reduce unintentional inputs and prevent
  dangerous actions. Use psychological constraints to
  improve the clarity and intuitiveness of a design.

See Also Affordance • Confirmation • Control • Errors
Forgiveness • Mapping • Nudge

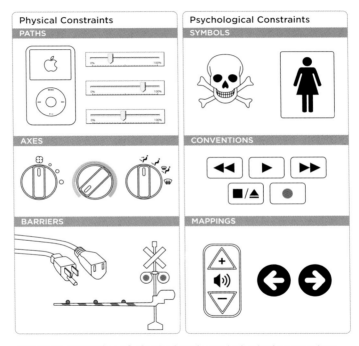

Common examples of physical and psychological constraints.

030

Contour Bias

A tendency to favor objects with contours over objects with sharp angles or points.

- Things that possess sharp angles or pointed features activate a region of the brain associated with fear.

- The bias likely evolved as a form of threat detection, enabling human ancestors to reflexively detect dangerous plants, animals, and objects.

- In neutral contexts, people prefer round, curvy objects to sharp, angular objects, but the latter is more effective at getting and holding attention.

- The degree of fear activation in the brain is proportionate to the sharpness of objects, and inversely related to object preference.

- Use angular and pointy features to attract and hold attention. Use contoured features to make a positive first impression. In emotionally neutral contexts, favor round, curvy forms over sharp, angular forms.

See Also   Affordance • Archetypes • Baby-Face Bias
Freeze-Flight-Fight-Forfeit • Threat Detection

The angular kettles are more effective at grabbing attention.
The contoured kettles are more emotionally appealing.

031

Control

The level of user control should be related to the proficiency and experience of the user.

- Novices perform best with less control, while experts perform best with more control. Accordingly, a well-designed system should offer varying levels of user control according to level of expertise.

- Novices benefit from structured interactions, minimal choices, prompts, constraints, and access to help.

- Experts benefit from less structure, direct access to functions, and minimal use of constraints and prompts.

- Since accommodating multiple methods increases complexity, the number of methods should be limited to two: one for beginners and one for experts.

- Provide methods optimized for beginners and experts for frequent operations. When systems are complex and frequently used, consider designs that can be customized to user preference and levels of expertise.

See Also   Constraint • Flexibility Trade-Offs • Visibility

The level of rider support decreases as expertise develops: from tricycle to training wheels to bicycle to Cirque du Soleil.

032

Convergence

A tendency for similar characteristics to evolve independently in similar environments.

- Environments influence which adaptive strategies are successful. Analogous environments result in analogous solutions to problems.

- It is common for discoveries and inventions to be made independently and simultaneously by multiple independent inventors and scientists.

- Stable environments promote convergence, favoring refinements to existing solutions.

- Volatile environments obstruct convergence, favoring innovation and experimentation.

- Consider convergence in innovation strategy, and as a reminder that others are likely working on ideas similar to yours right now.

See Also Iteration • Mimicry • Most Advanced Yet Acceptable

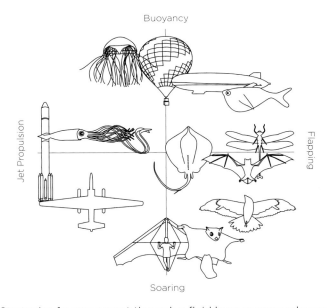

Buoyancy

Jet Propulsion

Flapping

Soaring

Strategies for movement through a fluid have converged over millions of years. This suggests that new systems will likely need to use one of these strategies to be competitive.

033

Cost-Benefit

The value of a thing is a function of its costs of acquisition and use versus the benefits it provides.

- Cost-benefit does not just refer to finances. It refers to all costs and benefits associated with a design, including physical costs (e.g., effort), emotional costs (e.g., frustration), and social costs (e.g., status).

- If the costs associated with a design outweigh the benefits, the design is poor. If the benefits outweigh the costs, the design is good.

- A common misconception is that adding features increases product value. This is only correct when the benefits provided by new features outweigh the costs of increased complexity. If they do not, adding features decreases product value.

- Consider the cost-benefit principle in all aspects of design. Do not make design decisions based on costs or benefits alone.

See Also 80/20 Rule • Feature Creep • IKEA Effect
Performance Load • Veblen Effect

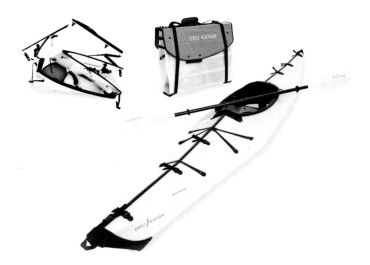

The hassles (i.e., cost) of transporting a kayak are high, which reduces the popularity of kayaking. Making the kayak more portable reduces this cost, making kayaking more appealing.

034

Crowd Intelligence

An emergent intelligence arising from the unwitting collaboration of many people.

- Crowd intelligence means that the average responses of a group to a certain class of problems are better than any individual response from that group. A crowd is any group of people whose members contribute independently to solving a problem.

- Crowd intelligence works best on problems that have definitive answers. For example, crowd intelligence is effective at solving math problems, but less effective at solving design problems.

- The highest crowd intelligence emerges from groups made up of diverse opinions and beliefs. Strong authoritative or social influences within a group undermines its crowd intelligence.

- Consider crowd intelligence as an alternative means of solving problems. Limit its use to problems that can be simply expressed and with definitive answers.

See Also   80/20 Rule • Normal Distribution • Selection Bias

Almost 800 people guessed the weight of an ox butchered and dressed. Statistician Francis Galton found that the average of these guesses missed the weight by only one pound, which was closer than any individual guess.

035

Defensible Space

An environment designed to deter crime through markers, surveillance, and signs of ownership.

- There are three key features of defensible spaces: territoriality, surveillance, and symbolic barriers.

- Territoriality refers to clearly defined spaces of ownership, like community markers, gates, walls, hedges, and fences.

- Surveillance refers to features that promote being seen, like external lighting, mailboxes located in well-trafficked areas, and well-maintained courtyards.

- Symbolic barriers refer to things that indicate ownership, like swings, flowers, and lawn furniture.

- Deter crime by marking territories to indicate ownership, increasing opportunities for surveillance, reducing features that allow concealment, and using symbolic barriers to indicate activity and use.

See Also   Affordance • Archetypes • Prospect-Refuge

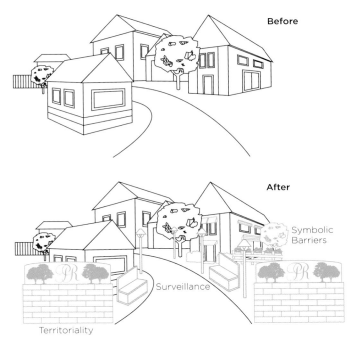

Before

After

Symbolic
Barriers

Surveillance

Territoriality

Deter neighborhood crime by adding territorial markers,
surveillance opportunities, and symbolic barriers.

036

Depth of Processing

Thinking hard about a thing improves the likelihood that it can be recalled.

- Information that is analyzed deeply is better recalled than information that is analyzed superficially.

- Memorization results from two types of rehearsal: maintenance and elaborative. Maintenance rehearsal involves repeating information back to yourself. Elaborative rehearsal involves deeper analysis, such as answering questions and creating analogies.

- Elaborative rehearsal results in recall that is two to three times better than maintenance rehearsal.

- The key factors determining recall are distinctiveness, relevance, and degree of elaborative rehearsal.

- Consider depth of processing when recall and retention are important. Get people to think hard about information by engaging them in different types of analysis. Use case studies, examples, and similar devices to make information interesting and relevant.

See Also   Serial Position Effects • von Restorff Effect

However, this bottle was not marked "poison," so Alice ventured to taste it, and finding it very nice (it had, in fact, a sort of mixed flavour of cherry-tart, custard, pineapple, roast turkey, coffee, and hot buttered toast), she very soon finished it off.

However, this bottle was not marked "poison," so Alice ventured to taste it, and finding it very nice (it had, in fact, a sort of mixed flavour of cherry-tart, custard, pineapple, roast turkey, coffee, and hot buttered toast), she very soon finished it off.

Information presented in a highly legible typeface (top) is easier to read, but less memorable than the same information in a less legible typeface (bottom). The reason? A typeface that is difficult to read makes readers think harder about the content, making it more memorable.

037

Design by Committee

A design process based on consensus building, group decision making, and extensive iteration.

- Design by committee is preferred when requirements are complex, consequences of error are serious, and stakeholder buy-in is important.

- Successful design committees are small and diverse, and equipped with the method to facilitate decision making and prevent deadlocks.

- Use design by committee when error mitigation and stakeholder acceptance are primary factors, and there is time for iteration. Use design by dictator when an aggressive time line is the primary concern.

- Autocracy is fast, but risky. Democracy is slow, but careful. Both models have their place depending on the circumstances.

See Also   Dunning-Kruger Effect • Feature Creep • Iteration
Not Invented Here • Prototyping

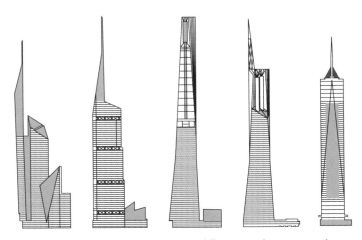

Design by committee averages out idiosyncrasies, as seen in the evolution (left to right) of One World Trade Center. The final design is less visually interesting, but overall it is superior because it better addresses all stakeholder requirements.

038

Desire Line

Traces of use or wear that indicate preferred methods of interaction.

- Desire lines generally refer to worn paths where people walk, but can be applied to any signs or traces left by user activity.

- Desire lines represent a noninvasive and unbiased measure of how people use things. For example, wear on computer keys indicates their frequency of use.

- Desire lines can be artificially created and studied using technologies such as video cameras, GPS, and website heat maps.

- Pay attention to desire lines. They indicate strong and unbiased user preferences, and represent opportunities for improvement.

See Also   Affordance • Cost-Benefit • Gamification
Performance Load • Root Cause

Desire lines are often seen branching off of designated paths, indicating a strong pedestrian preference for alternate routes.

039

Development Cycle

The stages of product creation: analysis, design, development, and testing.

- Analysis identifies and documents needs, resulting in a requirements document. Needs are discovered through research, customer feedback, focus groups, and direct experience with the problem.

- Design transforms the requirements into visual form, which becomes the specification. Design involves user research, ideation, prototyping, and testing.

- Development is where the design specification is transformed into an actual product.

- Testing ensures that a product meets both the requirements and design specification.

- Establish iterative development cycles, meaning that there is back and forth between groups at each stage. Work together to modify requirements and specifications as needed.

See Also Design by Committee • Hierarchy of Needs • Iteration
KISS • Life Cycle • Prototyping

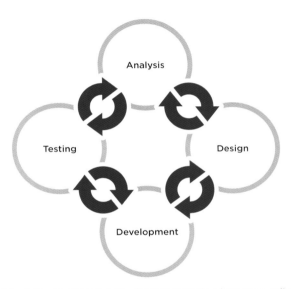

The ideal development cycle fosters iteration between adjacent stages in the cycle—and, as needed, nonadjacent stages.

040

Dunning-Kruger Effect

A tendency for unskilled people to overestimate their competence and performance.

- Incompetent people lack the knowledge and experience to recognize their own incompetence, as well as the competence of others.

- This creates a vicious cycle: An incompetent person can't perceive their own incompetence because they are incompetent; and overcoming incompetence requires the ability to distinguish skill levels, which is an ability they lack.

- Conversely, highly competent people tend to underestimate their abilities and performance, and overestimate the skills of others.

- Combat the Dunning-Kruger effect by teaching the inexperienced how to discern competence from incompetence. Provide regular feedback and critiques to promote the development of self-assessment skills.

See Also Crowd Intelligence • Design by Committee
Hanlon's Razor • Not Invented Here

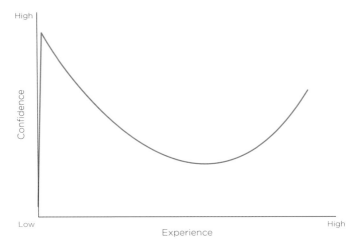

The least competent tend to be the most confident, and then the roller coaster ride of reality begins.

041

Entry Point

A point of physical or attentional entry that sets the emotional tone for subsequent interactions.

- Good entry points feature three elements: minimal barriers, points of prospect, and progressive lures.

- Barriers should not encumber entry points. Examples include highly trafficked parking lots, noisy displays, and salespeople standing at the doors.

- Entry points enable people to survey available options. Examples include entrances that provide a clear view of store layout, and web pages that provide orientation cues and visible navigation options.

- Progressive lures pull people through the entry point. Examples include jumplines in newspapers and compelling displays just beyond the entry of a store.

- Optimize entry points by reducing barriers, establishing clear points of prospect, and using progressive lures.

See Also   Desire Lines • Prospect-Refuge • Wayfinding

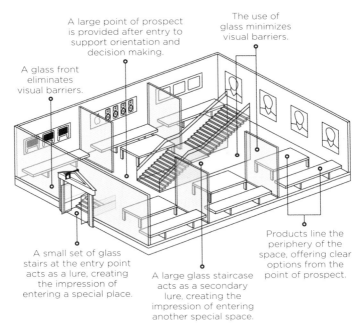

A large point of prospect is provided after entry to support orientation and decision making.

The use of glass minimizes visual barriers.

A glass front eliminates visual barriers.

A small set of glass stairs at the entry point acts as a lure, creating the impression of entering a special place.

A large glass staircase acts as a secondary lure, creating the impression of entering another special space.

Products line the periphery of the space, offering clear options from the point of prospect.

Apple retail stores have redefined the retail experience, in part due to their exceptional entry-point experience design.

042

Errors

An action or omission of action yielding an unintended result.

- There are three categories of error: slips, mistakes, and lapses.

- Slips occur when an action is not what was intended; for example, when a person intends to press one button but accidentally presses another.

- Mistakes occur when an intention is incorrect; for example, when a nurse interprets an alarm incorrectly and then administers the wrong medicine.

- Lapses occur when an action is forgotten for example, when a pilot forgets to lower landing gear for landing.

- Minimize slips using affordances, confirmations, and constraints. Minimize mistakes using clear feedback, mappings, and training. Minimize lapses using alarms, checklists, and visibility.

See Also   Affordance • Confirmation • Constraint • Visibility

Texting Slip

Texting Mistake

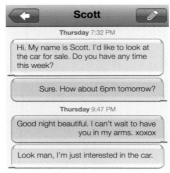

Texting Lapse

043

Expectation Effects

Changes in perception or behavior resulting from personal expectations or expectations of others.

- When people have expectations about something, it influences how they perceive and react to that thing.

- For example, students perform better or worse based on the expressed expectations of their teachers. And patients experience treatment effects based on their belief that a treatment will or will not work.

- These effects create challenges for direct measurement techniques, such as focus groups, interviews, and surveys.

- Consider expectation effects when conducting research, interviews, and testing. Favor blinded experiments and noninvasive research such as field observation over invasive methods. In persuasion contexts, set expectations in a credible fashion versus letting people form their own unbiased conclusions.

See Also   Affordance • Confirmation Bias • Framing
Mere-Exposure Effect • Uncertainty Principle

A taste test between two wines: an inexpensive wine in cheap packaging and an expensive wine in fancy packaging. People rate the expensive wine as tasting better—even when the wines are the same.

044

Face-ism Ratio

The ratio of face to body in an image that influences how the person is perceived.

- The face-ism ratio is calculated by dividing the head height by the total visible body height.

- Images depicting a person with a high face-ism ratio—i.e., the face takes up most of the image—focus attention on the person's intellect and personality.

- Images depicting a person with a low face-ism ratio—i.e., the body takes up most of the image—focus attention on the person's body and sexuality.

- When a design requires a thoughtful response, use images of people with high face-ism ratios. When a design requires an emotional response, use images with low-face-ism ratios.

See Also   Attractiveness Bias • Baby-Face Bias
Classical Conditioning • Law of Prägnanz

Face-ism Ratio = .96

Face-ism Ratio = .55

Face-ism Ratio = .37

The high face-ism ratio image emphasizes attributes like intelligence and ambition. The lower face-ism ratio images emphasize attributes like sexuality and physical attractiveness.

045

Factor of Safety

The design of a system beyond expected loads to offset the effects of unknown variables and prevent failure.

- Increasing the factor of safety of a design is a reliable method of preventing catastrophic failure.

- The size of the factor of safety should correspond to the level of uncertainty in the design parameters. High uncertainty requires a high factor of safety.

- New designs use high factors of safety because uncertainty is high. The focus is on survivability.

- Tried-and-true designs use low factors of safety because more is known. The focus shifts to cost.

- Use factors of safety in proportion to your knowledge of the design parameters and the severity of the consequences of failure.

See Also   Design by Committee • Errors • Modularity
Structural Forms • Weakest Link

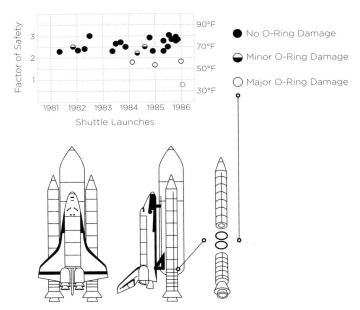

The O-rings of Challenger's solid rocket boosters had a factor of safety of three—inadequate for low temperature conditions. Catastrophic failure occurred shortly after launch in 1986.

046

Feature Creep

A continuous expansion or addition of new product features.

- Feature creep is one of the most common causes of cost and schedule overruns. This occurs because features are easy or convenient to add, accumulate over multiple generations of a product, or are added to appease internal project stakeholders.

- The key driver is the perception that more is better, and therefore features are continuously added and rarely taken away. But adding features adds complexity, and complexity is expensive.

- Beware feature creep in design and development. Ensure features are linked to customer needs, and are not added out of convenience or appeasement. Create a milestone to formally freeze the product specification, and shout "feature creeper" at any person attempting to add features beyond that point.

See Also 80/20 Rule • Design by Committee • KISS

On its maiden voyage in 1628, the Swedish warship Vasa sank after going less than one mile. The cause? Extra guns, decks, and carvings added during construction compromised its stability. Feature creep literally sank the ship.

047

Feedback Loop

A cycle in which output feeds back into a system as input, changing subsequent output.

- A feedback loop is a cause-and-effect chain that forms a loop. There are two types of feedback loops: positive and negative.

- Positive feedback loops amplify output, resulting in accelerated growth or decline. Therefore, positive feedback can be useful for creating rapid change, but perilous because it is difficult to arrest.

- Negative feedback loops dampen output, resulting in equilibrium around a point. Therefore, negative feedback can be useful for stabilization, but perilous because it can be difficult to change.

- Use positive feedback to create change, but include negative feedback to prevent runaway effects. Use negative feedback to resist change, but note that too much negative feedback leads to stagnation.

See Also   Iteration • Root Cause • Shaping • Social Trap

Bridges resist dynamic loads using structures and materials that create negative feedback. But the negative feedback built into the 1940 Tacoma Narrows Bridge was no match for the positive feedback between the bridge's deflection and the wind. The bridge collapsed five months after it opened.

048

Fibonacci Sequence

A sequence of numbers that form patterns
commonly found in nature.

- A Fibonacci sequence is a sequence of numbers in
  which each number is the sum of the two preceding
  numbers (e.g., 1, 1, 2, 3, 5, 8, 13...).

- Patterns exhibiting the sequence are commonly found
  in nature, such as flower petals, spirals of galaxies, and
  bones in the human hand, and as such, are conjectured
  to represent proportions with universal appeal.

- The division of any two adjacent numbers in a
  Fibonacci sequence yields an approximation of the
  golden ratio. Approximations are rough for early
  numbers in the sequence but increasingly accurate as
  the sequence progresses.

- Consider Fibonacci sequences when developing
  compositions, geometric patterns, and organic motifs,
  especially when they involve rhythms and harmonies
  among multiple elements.

See Also   Golden Ratio • Self-Similarity • Wabi-Sabi

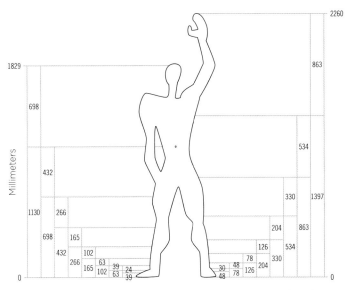

Le Corbusier derived two Fibonacci sequences based on key features of the human form to create the Modulor, a model used to optimize spaces for humans.

049

Figure-Ground

Elements are perceived as either figures (objects of focus) or ground (the rest of the perceptual field).

- One of the Gestalt principles of perception.

- The human perceptual system separates stimuli into figure elements or ground elements. Figure elements receive more attention and are better remembered than ground elements.

- Elements below a horizon line or in the lower regions of a design are more likely to be perceived as figures.

- Elements above a horizon line or in the upper region are more likely to be perceived as ground.

- Increase the recall of key elements by making them figures in a composition. Clearly differentiate between figure and ground elements to focus attention and minimize perceptual confusion.

See Also 3D Projection • Closure • Signal-to-Noise Ratio

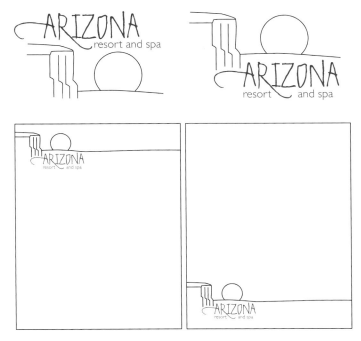

Placing elements below a horizon line or at the bottom of a page makes them figures, which makes them more memorable.

050

Fitts' Law

The time required to touch a target is a function of the target size and the distance to the target.

- Proposed by American psychologist Paul Fitts.

- Used to model pointing to an object or computer screen using your finger or pointing device.

- The law is predictive over a wide variety of conditions, devices, and people.

- The primary implication of Fitts' law is that close, large targets can be accessed more quickly and with fewer errors than distant, small targets.

- Constraints can effectively increase target size. For example, a dropdown menu located at the top of a computer display effectively has infinite height because the screen edge stops the cursor.

- Consider Fitts' Law when designing controls and control layouts. Keep controls close and large when speed or accuracy is important.

See Also Constraints • Errors • Hick's Law • Performance Load

The time and error rate involved in whacking a mole is a function of the distance between the whacker and the mole.

051

Five Hat Racks

A metaphor representing the five ways information can be organized.

- Information can be organized by category, time, location, alphabet, and continuum.

- Category refers to organization by similarity or relatedness; for example, a store organizing products by aisle or a library organizing books by subject.

- Time refers to organization by chronological order; for example, timelines and TV guide schedules.

- Location refers to organization by geographical or spatial reference; for example, emergency exit maps and travel guides.

- Alphabet refers to organization by alphabetical sequence; for example, dictionaries and this book.

- Continuum refers to organization by magnitude; for example, baseball batting averages and search results.

See Also   Framing • Hierarchy • Layering • Similarity

ALPHABETICAL NAME

Beagle · Bulldog · German Shepherd · Golden Retriever · Labrador Retriever · Yorkshire Terrier

TIME RECOGNITION

1885 Beagle · 1885 Yorkshire Terrier · 1886 Bulldog · 1908 German Shepherd · 1917 Labrador Retriever · 1925 Golden Retriever

LOCATION COUNTRY

CANADA — Labrador Retriever

ENGLAND — Beagle · Bulldog · Yorkshire Terrier

GERMANY — German Shepherd

SCOTLAND — Golden Retriever

CONTINUUM POPULARITY

1 Labrador Retriever · 2 German Shepherd · 3 Golden Retriever · 4 Beagle · 5 Bulldog · 6 Yorkshire Terrier

CATEGORY GROUP

SPORTING — Labrador Retriever · Golden Retriever

HERDING — German Shepherd

HOUND — Beagle

NON WORKING — Bulldog

TOY — Yorkshire Terrier

Six breeds of dog organized using the five hat racks. Note how the method of organization influences the story the data tell.

052

Flexibility Trade-Offs

As the flexibility of a design increases, the usability and performance of the design decreases.

- Accommodating flexibility entails satisfying a larger set of design requirements, which invariably means more compromises and complexity in design.

- Increasing complexity generally decreases performance and usability.

- For example, the Swiss Army knife has many tools that increase its flexibility, but the tools are less efficient and less usable than their standalone equivalents. Performance and usability are traded for flexibility.

- Specialized things outperform flexible things when their requirements are stable. Flexible things outperform specialized things when their requirements are volatile.

- When flexibility is key, prepare to compromise performance and usability. When performance or usability is key, prepare to compromise flexibility.

See Also Cost-Benefit • Feature Creep • Hick's Law

The Swiss Army knife is a prime example of flexibility trade-offs. It is the proverbial "Jack of all trades, master of none".

053

Flow

A state of immersion so intense that awareness of the real world is lost.

- When people are not challenged, they become bored. When they are challenged too much, they become frustrated. Flow occurs when people are challenged at or near their maximum skill level.

- People in a state of flow lose track of time and experience feelings of joy and satisfaction.

- Tasks that create flow experiences have achievable goals, require continuous engagement, provide clear and immediate feedback, and are able to maintain a balance between difficulty and skill level.

- Incorporate elements of flow in activities that seek to engage the attention of people over time—e.g., instruction, games, and music. Designing tasks to achieve flow is more art than science; therefore, leave ample time for experimentation and tuning.

See Also Control • Gamification • Performance Load
Progressive Disclosure • Zeigarnik Effect

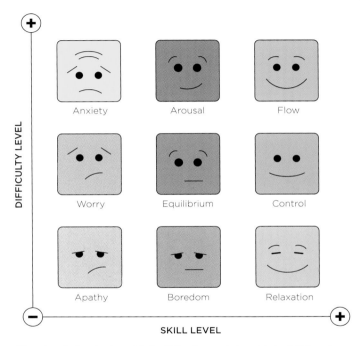

Flow is attained when high difficulty matches high skill level.

054

Forgiveness

Designs should help people avoid errors, and protect them from harm when they do occur.

- Forgiving design prevents errors through constraints and good affordances.

- Forgiving design warns of potential dangers, and asks for confirmation when choices may cause harm.

- Forgiving design allows actions to be reversible when errors do occur (e.g., undo function).

- Forgiving design provides safety nets to prevent harm resulting from errors or catastrophic failures.

- Make all designs forgiving. Best to prevent errors, then to warn of potential errors, then to reverse errors when they occur, and then when all else fails to have safety nets in place. To err is human, to forgive, design.

See Also   Affordance • Confirmation • Constraint • Errors
Factor of Safety • Weakest Link

When all else fails, what pilot and crew wouldn't want this ballistic recovery system as a safety net of last resort?

055

Form Follows Function

Aesthetic considerations should be secondary to functional considerations.

- A maxim derived from the architect Louis Sullivan, who wrote that, in nature, "form ever follows function".

- The motto became a guiding principle for modernists who emphasized function over ornamentation.

- The prescriptive interpretation means that designers should focus on function first, form second. The descriptive interpretation means that beauty arises from purity of function.

- Though the maxim is often considered oversimple and cliché, most great designers abide by the principle.

- Consider form follows function a strong guideline in design. While it does not apply to all cases all of the time, it generally leads to superior design.

See Also 80/20 Rule • KISS • MAYA • Ockham's Razor

The Jeep is the embodiment of form follows function. General Eisenhower identified it as one of three tools that won WWII.

056

Framing

A method of presenting choices in specific ways to influence decision making and judgment.

- Framing is the structuring of words and images to influence how people think and feel about something, typically to influence a decision or judgment.

- For example, a frozen yogurt that is advertised to be "95% fat-free" elicits a positive emotional response, whereas a frozen yogurt advertised to be "5% fat" elicits a negative emotional response, even though the two statements are logically equivalent.

- Frames that emphasize benefits are most effective for audiences focused on aspiration and pleasure seeking. Frames that emphasize losses are most effective for audiences focused on security and pain avoidance.

- Consider framing to influence decision making and judgment. Use the appropriate type of framing for an audience, ensuring that frames do not conflict.

See Also Expectation Effects • Mere-Exposure Effect

The Ohio Dry Campaign of 1918 is a case study in framing: Are you for the defenders of freedom, or are you for the booze?

057

Freeze-Flight-Fight-Forfeit

The ordered, instinctive response to acute stress.

- When people are exposed to stressful or threatening situations, their instinctive responses are to freeze, flee, fight, and forfeit, in that order.

- When a threat is suspected, the instinctive response is to freeze—to stop, look, and listen for threats.

- When a threat is detected, the instinctive response is to flee—to escape from the threat.

- When unable to escape from a threat, the instinctive response is to fight—to neutralize the threat.

- When unable to neutralize the threat, the instinctive response is to forfeit—to surrender to the threat.

- Consider freeze-flight-fight-forfeit in the design of systems that involve performance under extreme stress. It is critical to design systems and training to address each stage of the stress response differently versus a one-strategy-fits-all approach.

See Also Classical Conditioning • Threat Detection

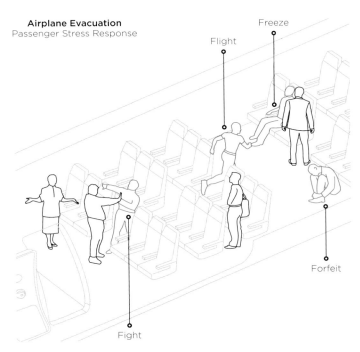

Airplane Evacuation
Passenger Stress Response

Flight

Freeze

Fight

Forfeit

People respond to extreme stress in four ways. It is important to design systems and training to address each of them.

058

Gamification

Using gaming strategies in nongame contexts to enhance experience and modify behavior.

- Gamification involves rewarding desired behaviors, providing frequent feedback, and illustrating achievements in highly visible ways.

- Key gamification principles include clearly defined goals, scorekeeping and scorecards, frequent feedback, free choice, and ample coaching.

- One model for determining rewards is called SAPS: status, access, power, and stuff. The model was proposed by Gabe Zichermann, and purports to list in order the things people most desire.

- Measure behaviors you want to increase and provide immediate visual feedback about that behavior. Consider the SAPS model in the design of rewards systems. Allow people to fail, then support the failure with coaching and instructional feedback.

See Also   Operant Conditioning • Shaping • Zeigarnik Effect

How do you get people to start taking the stairs in Sweden?
Convert the stairs into a piano that plays music with each step.

059

Garbage In-Garbage Out

The quality of system output is largely dependent on the quality of system input.

- The "garbage in" metaphor refers to two categories of input problems: type and quality.

- Problems of type occur when the wrong type of input is provided; for example, entering a phone number into a credit card number field.

- Problems of quality occur when the correct type of input is provided, but with defects; for example, entering a phone number into a phone number field, but entering it incorrectly.

- Avoid garbage-out by preventing garbage-in. Use affordances and constraints to minimize problems of type. Use previews and confirmations to minimize problems of quality.

See Also Affordance • Confirmation • Constraint • Errors
Feedback Loop • Signal-to-Noise Ratio

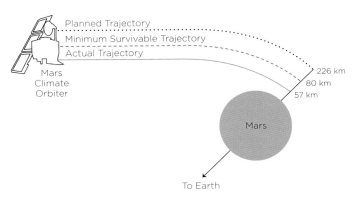

The Mars Climate Orbiter disintegrated in the Martian atmosphere in 1999. The cause? Garbage in-garbage out. Trajectory corrections were entered in English units versus the required metric units, dooming the craft.

060

Gloss Bias

A preference for glossy versus dull objects.

- People find glossy objects more interesting and appealing than dull objects.

- For example, people generally prefer glossy lipsticks, jewelry, paper, and paints to their matte counterparts. Young children presented with glossy objects lick them significantly more than dull objects.

- The preference is likely an evolutionary artifact. The ability to find water sources provided early human ancestors with an adaptive advantage. Glossy surfaces suggested nearby water sources.

- Consider the gloss bias when selecting finishes. The bias applies to all objects and images of objects. The bias is stronger in general audiences, and weaker in audiences with experience with different finishes.

See Also   Archetypes • Biophilia Effect • Savanna Preference
Scarcity • Supernormal Stimulus

Humans have evolved to find glossy things appealing. You might even say we thirst for them.

061

Golden Ratio

A ratio within the elements of a form, such as height to width, approximating 0.618.

- The golden ratio is commonly believed to be an aesthetically pleasing proportion, primarily due to its unique mathematical properties, prevalence in nature, and use in great artistic and architectural works.

- The prevalence of golden proportions over other proportions may, however, be illusory—a result of cherry-picked evidence and confirmation bias.

- Psychological evidence supporting a preference for golden proportions over other proportions is weak. If a preference exists, it is small.

- Explore golden ratio proportions in your designs, but not at the expense of other design objectives.

See Also Confirmation Bias • Fibonacci Sequence
Rule of Thirds • Selection Bias • Waist-to-Hip Ratio

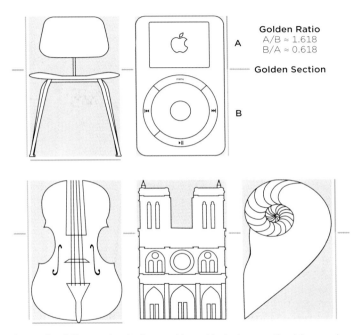

Golden Ratio
A/B ≈ 1.618
B/A ≈ 0.618

Golden Section

A

B

In each of these classic forms, the ratio between the blue and red segments approximates the Golden ratio.

062

Good Continuation

The tendency to perceive lines as continuing their established directions.

- One of the Gestalt principles of perception.

- Things arranged in a straight line or a smooth curve are perceived as a unit, making them easier to visually process and remember. The line is perceived to continue in its established direction.

- When sections of a line or shape are hidden from view, good continuation leads the eye to continue along the visible segments. If extensions of these segments intersect with minimal disruption, the elements along the line are perceived to be related. As the angle of disruption becomes more acute, the elements are perceived to be less related.

- Use good continuation to indicate relatedness between elements in a design. Arrange elements in graphs and displays such that end points of elements form continuous, rather than abrupt lines.

See Also Alignment • Area Alignment • Chunking • Closure
Similarity • Uniform Connectedness

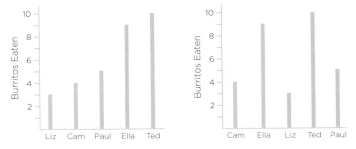

The first graph is easier to read than the second because the end points of its bars form a line that is more continuous.

063

Green Effects

A set of cognitive and behavioral effects triggered by exposure to the color green.

- Green is universally associated with safety and security, perhaps a vestige of our arboreal ancestry, and the reason that green traffic lights around the globe mean "go". Additionally, green is associated with nature and sustainability.

- Green environments reduce stress and mental fatigue, and promote problem solving and creativity.

- Green apparel tends to negatively impact physical attractiveness. For example, a person in green is rated less attractive than all other colors except yellow.

- Use green to promote associations with nature and sustainability. Use green when creating signage and controls to indicate safe passage. Consider green interiors to reduce stress and promote creativity.

See Also   Biophilia Effect • Gloss Bias • Prospect-Refuge Savanna Preference • Yellow Effects

A hospital hall redesigned with ample greenery to comfort patients as they move from the lobby to their destination.

064

Gutenberg Diagram

A diagram that describes the pattern followed by the eyes when looking at a page of information.

- Western cultures read displays from top-left to bottom-right, sweeping from left to right as they progress. The tendency to follow this path is described as "reading gravity".

- Layouts that follow the diagram and work in harmony with reading gravity purportedly improve reading rhythm and comprehension, though there is little empirical evidence to support this.

- The Gutenberg diagram is only predictive of eye movement for homogeneous displays of information.

- Consider the Gutenberg diagram in layout and composition when elements are evenly distributed. Otherwise, use the weight and composition of elements to lead the eye.

See Also   Alignment • Entry Point • Progressive Disclosure
Readability • Serial Position Effects

CHAPTER 1: Down the Rabbit-Hole

Alice was beginning to get very tired of sitting by her sister on the bank, and of having nothing to do: once or twice she had peeped into the book her sister was reading, but it had no pictures or conversations in it, 'and what is the use of a book,' thought Alice 'without pictures or conversation?'

So she was considering in her own mind (as well as she could, for the hot day made her feel very sleepy and stupid), whether the pleasure of making a daisy-chain would be worth the trouble of getting up and picking the daisies, when suddenly a White Rabbit with pink eyes ran close by her.

There was nothing so very remarkable in that; nor did Alice think it so very much out of the way to hear the Rabbit say to itself, 'Oh dear! Oh dear! I shall be late!' (when she thought it over afterwards, it occurred to her that she ought to have wondered at this, but at the time it all seemed quite natural); but when the Rabbit actually took a watch out of its waistcoat-pocket, and looked at it, and then hurried on, Alice started to her feet, for it flashed across her mind that she had never before seen a rabbit with either a waistcoat-pocket, or a watch to take out of it, and burning with curiosity, she ran across the field after it, and fortunately was just in time to see it pop down a large rabbit-hole under the hedge.

In another moment down went Alice after it, never once considering how in the world she was to get out again.

The rabbit-hole went straight on like a tunnel for some way, and then dipped suddenly down, so suddenly that Alice had not a moment to think about stopping herself before she found herself falling down a very deep well.

Either the well was very deep, or she fell very slowly, for she had plenty of time as she went down to look about her and to wonder what was going to happen next. First, she tried to look down and make out what she was coming to, but it was too dark to see anything; then she looked at the sides of the well, and noticed that they were filled with cupboards and book-shelves; here and there she saw maps and pictures hung upon pegs.

Compositions that follow the Gutenberg diagram position key elements diagonally from top-left to bottom-right.

065

Hanlon's Razor

Never attribute to malice what can be adequately explained by incompetence.

- Proposed both by Robert Hanlon and science fiction author Robert Heinlein.

- A variant of Ockham's razor, Hanlon's razor asserts that when bad things happen that are human-caused, it is far more likely to be the result of ignorance or bureaucracy than conspiracy or malice.

- For example, when Apple's Siri search was unable to find abortion clinics, many claimed Apple purposefully excluded them from the search results. The more likely explanation is that Siri was incomplete or buggy.

- Keep Hanlon's razor in mind when bad things happen. The principle does not exclude the possibility of malice—sometimes bad things are, in fact, caused by bad people—but malice is generally less probable.

See Also   Affordance • Black Effects • Contour Bias
Mimicry • Supernormal Stimulus • Threat Detection

What caused the post-Katrina New Orleans levees to fail? Inadequate engineering is more likely than government conspiracy—though, the government did blow up the levees in 1927 under similar circumstances.

Hick's Law

The time it takes to make a decision increases with
the number of options.

- Proposed by British psychologist W.E. Hick.

- Hick's Law applies to simple decisions with multiple
  options. For example, if A happens, then push button
  1; If B happens, then push button 2.

- Increasing the number of choices increases decision
  time logarithmically.

- Hick's Law does not apply to complex decision
  making, or decisions requiring reading, scanning,
  searching, or extended deliberation.

- Consider Hick's Law in designs that involve simple
  decision making. Reduce the number of options to
  reduce response times and errors.

See Also Chunking • Errors • Fitts' Law • Interference Effects
Signal-to-Noise Ratio • Wayfinding

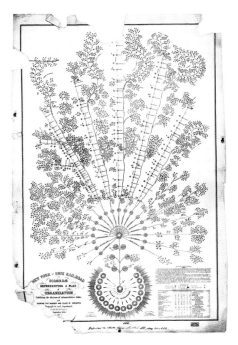

This classic 1855 organizational chart of the New York and Erie Railroad uses a tree structure with elements of stairs and nests.

Hierarchy of Needs

The user-centered goals that a design must satisfy in order to achieve optimal success.

- The hierarchy of needs consists of five levels that are typically satisfied in sequence:

  1. Functionality: fosters satisfaction by meeting basic functional needs.

  2. Reliability: fosters trust through consistent and reliable performance over time.

  3. Usability: fosters fondness through ease of use.

  4. Proficiency: fosters pride and status through increased productivity and empowerment.

  5. Creativity: fosters cultlike loyalty through innovation and personal enrichment.

- Consider the hierarchy of needs in design strategy. Markets with products low on the hierarchy are ripe for disruption; whereas markets with products high on the hierarchy will be the most competitive.

See Also   Aesthetic-Usability Effect • Form Follows Function

GoPro cameras were designed to be small and rugged, but who could have anticipated the creativity they would unleash?

069

Highlighting

A technique for focusing attention on an area of text or image.

- Highlighting focuses attention by varying elements (e.g., capitalization) or adding elements (e.g., color).

- Highlight no more than 10 percent of a visible display. When everything is highlighted, nothing is highlighted.

- Use bold to highlight titles, labels, and short word sequences. Use italics and uppercase text for more subtle highlighting. Use underlining sparingly, if at all.

- Use color to highlight long word sequences. Ensure high contrast when using color to highlight.

- Animation such as blinking is a powerful means of attracting attention. Accordingly, it should only be used for alert-type information that requires an immediate response. It is important to be able to turn off the animation once it is acknowledged, as it distracts from other tasks.

See Also   Interference Effects • Layering • von Restorff Effect

BOLD

Chapter 8

The Queen turned **crimson** with fury, and, after glaring at her for a moment like a wild beast, **screamed** "Off with her head! Off—"

UPPERCASE AND ITALICS

CHAPTER 8

The Queen turned *crimson* with fury, and, after glaring at her for a moment like a wild beast, *screamed* "Off with her head! Off—"

COLOR

Chapter 8

The Queen turned crimson with fury, and, after glaring at her for a moment like a wild beast, screamed "Off with her head! Off—"

070

Horror Vacui

A tendency to fill blank spaces with things rather than leaving spaces empty.

- A Latin expression meaning "fear of emptiness".

- Though the term has varied meanings dating back to Aristotle, today it is principally used to describe a style of art and design that leaves no empty space.

- The style is commonly employed in commercial media such as newspapers, comic books, and websites.

- As horror vacui increases, perceived value decreases.

- For example, the number of products in retail windows tends to be inversely related to the average price of products and store brand prestige.

- Consider horror vacui in the design of commercial displays and advertising. Favor minimalism to signal high-priced products. Favor horror vacui to signal low-priced products.

See Also   Inattentional Blindness • Left-Digit Effect
Ockham's Razor • Signal-to-Noise Ratio

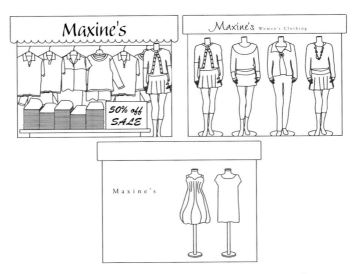

The perceived value of a store's merchandise in a storefront window is inversely related to its horror vacui.

071

Hunter-Nurturer Bias

A tendency for male children to be interested in hunting-related things and female children to be interested in nurturing-related things.

- Male children tend to engage in play that emulates hunting behaviors. Female children tend to engage in play that emulates nurturing behaviors.

- Hunter bias is characterized by activities involving object movement and location, weapons and tools, hunting and fighting, predators, and physical play.

- Nurturer bias is characterized by activities involving form and colors, facial expressions and interpersonal skills, caretaking, babies, and verbal play.

- Consider hunter-nurturer bias when designing for children. Consider hunting-related items and activities for male children, and nurturer-related items and activities for female children.

See Also   Archetypes • Baby-Face Bias • Contour Bias
Supernormal Stimulus • Threat Detection

Like their human cousins, female vervets prefer stereotypically female toys and male vervets prefer stereotypically male toys.

072

Iconic Representation

The use of pictorial images to improve recognition and recall.

- There are four kinds of icons: resemblance, exemplar, symbolic, and arbitrary.

- Resemblance icons look like the things they portray.

- Exemplar icons are examples of things.

- Symbolic icons make use of familiar symbols.

- Arbitrary icons are used to establish industry standards or international communication.

- Consider iconic representation to aid recognition and recall, overcome language barriers, and enhance the aesthetics of communication. Generally, icons should be labeled and share a common visual motif for optimal performance.

See Also   Chunking • Performance Load
Picture Superiority Effect • Rosetta Stone

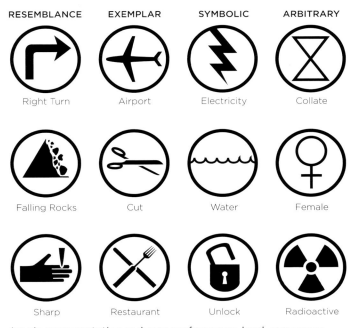

RESEMBLANCE — Right Turn
EXEMPLAR — Airport
SYMBOLIC — Electricity
ARBITRARY — Collate
Falling Rocks
Cut
Water
Female
Sharp
Restaurant
Unlock
Radioactive

Iconic representation reduces performance load, conserves display area, and is more understandable across cultures.

073

IKEA Effect

The act of creating a thing increases the perceived value of that thing to the creator.

- Creating or partially creating a thing (e.g., assembling furniture) makes it more valuable to the creator.

- People are willing to pay more for products they create than equivalent preassembled products.

- People value things they personally create as much as if it had been created by an expert.

- The level of effort invested in creation corresponds to its level of valuation: high effort translates into high valuation, and low effort translates into low valuation.

- The IKEA effect only holds when tasks are completed.

- Consider the IKEA effect in product strategy and user-experience design. Engage users in the creation of products to increase their value perception.

See Also   Closure • Cognitive Dissonance • Not Invented Here
Sunk Cost Effect • Zeigarnik Effect

The effort people expend when assembling IKEA furniture actually makes them value the furniture more.

074

Inattentional Blindness

A failure to perceive an unexpected stimulus presented in clear view.

- When concentrating on tasks, people are blind to unrelated stimuli up to 50 percent of the time.

- For example, a shopper seeking a certain brand of soda will likely notice other soda bottles, but not dishwasher soap bottles.

- Inattentional blindness is behind many of the tricks and misdirections employed by magicians.

- Consider inattentional blindness in contexts where attention is key, including security, safety, and advertising. Given the robustness of the effect, the best strategy is to create or alter tasks to focus attention on desired stimuli (e.g., receiving a coupon book prior to visiting a store can predefine the shopping targets ahead of time).

See Also Flow • Interference Effects • Signal-to-Noise Ratio

When people were asked to count the number of times the team in the white shirts passed a basketball, half failed to see the person in a gorilla costume casually stroll across the screen.

075

Interference Effects

Things that trigger conflicting thought processes reduce thinking efficiency.

- Interference effects occur when nonessential mental processes interfere with essential mental processes, increasing errors and slowing task performance.

- Nonessential mental processes can be triggered by conflicting meanings, distractions in the environment, and memories that are irrelevant to the task at hand.

- For example, a green "stop" button triggers a mental process for "go" because of the color green, and a mental process for "stop" because of the label "stop". The two mental processes interfere with one another.

- Minimize interference by eliminating elements that distract. Keep designs simple. Abide by strong color and symbol conventions when they exist (e.g., red means stop, green means go).

See Also   Errors • Inattentional Blindness • Performance Load

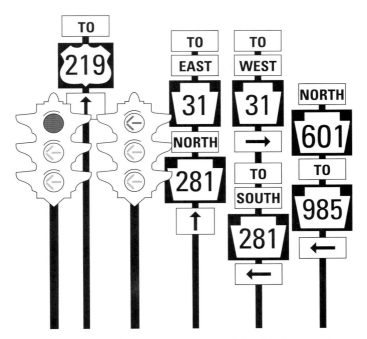

Arrows mean "go", but red arrows mean "stop". When traffic signs and signals create interference, accidents increase.

076

Inverted Pyramid

Information presented in order of importance—
from most important to least important.

- In the pyramid metaphor, the base represents the
  most important information, while the tip represents
  the least important information. To invert the pyramid
  is to present the important information first, and the
  background information last.

- The inverted pyramid has been a standard in
  journalism for over one hundred years, and has found
  wide use in instructional design and technical writing.

- The lead is the critical component of the inverted
  pyramid, as it is presented first. It should be a terse
  summary of the what, where, when, who, and why.

- Use the inverted pyramid when presentation efficiency
  is important. When it is not possible to use the
  inverted pyramid (e.g., scientific writing), consider an
  abstract or executive summary at the beginning to
  present the key findings.

See Also Progressive Disclosure • Serial Position Effects

LEAD
Information Readers Must Have To Know What Happened

This evening at about 9:30 PM, at Ford's Theater, the President, while sitting in his private box with Mrs. Lincoln, Miss Harris, and Major Rathbone, was shot by an assassin who suddenly entered the box and approached the President.

BODY
Information That Helps Readers
Understand But Isn't Essential

General Grant and wife were advertised to be at the theater this evening, but he started for Burlington at six o'clock this evening. At a cabinet meeting at which General Grant was present, the subject of the state of the country, and the prospect of a speedy peace was discussed.

CONCLUSION
Information
That's Interesting
Or Nice to Have

All the members of the cabinet, except Mr. Seward, are now in attendance upon the President. I have seen Mr. Seward, but he and Frederick are both unconscious.

The report of President Lincoln's assassination established the inverted pyramid style of writing in 1865.

077

Iteration

Repeating a set of design and development operations, with each repetition building on the last, until the desired result is achieved.

- Complexity does not emerge without iteration. In nature, iteration allows complex structures to form by progressively building on simpler structures.

- Design iteration refers to repeating the basic steps of analysis, prototyping, and testing until a desired result is achieved.

- With iterative design, there is no failure—just iterations with lessons learned to apply to the next iteration. Accordingly, failure is not to be feared but embraced.

- Iteration is the backbone of design and design thinking. Great design does not happen without it.

- Embrace iteration in all aspects of design and development. Seek ways to accelerate iteration to speed learning and progress. Fail fast. Fail early.

See Also Development Cycle • Feedback Loop • KISS
Prototyping • Self-Similarity

By focusing on designing a plane that could be rebuilt in hours versus months, engineer Paul MacCready enabled his team to dramatically speed up iteration. Six months later, the Gossamer Condor flew over 2,000 meters, winning the first Kremer Prize.

078

KISS

Simple designs work better and are more reliable.

- The acronym KISS—"keep it simple stupid"—was proposed by Kelly Johnson, lead engineer at the Lockheed Skunk Works.

- KISS asserts that simple systems typically work better than complex systems. Accordingly, simplicity should be a key goal in design.

- Simplicity means minimal elements with the minimal interactions between those elements.

- Simple designs are typically faster and cheaper to build, perform more reliably, and are easier to troubleshoot and maintain.

- KISS is commonly employed in engineering and software development, but is applicable to any field that makes things, from entrepreneurship to writing.

- Keep it simple stupid.

See Also 80/20 Rule • Feature Creep • Form Follows Function
Modularity • Ockham's Razor

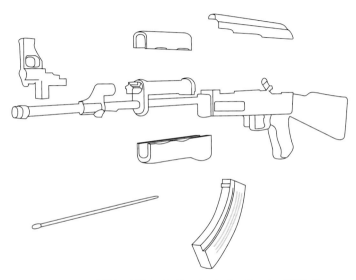

A testament to Mikhail Kalashnikov's dedication to KISS, the AK-47 is perhaps the least expensive and most reliable assault rifle ever produced. It has only eight moving parts.

079

Law of Prägnanz

A tendency to interpret images as simple and complete versus complex and incomplete.

- One of the Gestalt principles of perception.

- When people are presented with a set of elements that can be interpreted in different ways, they tend to assume the simplest interpretation.

- For example, the characters :-) are interpreted as a smiling face versus three separate characters.

- The law applies similarly to the way in which images are recalled from memory. For example, people recall the positions of countries on maps as more aligned and symmetrical than they are in reality.

- Generally, people are better able to interpret and remember simple figures than complex figures.

- Consider the Law of Prägnanz when depicting and interpreting images. Favor simplicity and symmetry to facilitate visual processing, and favor complexity and asymmetry to impede visual processing.

See Also   Closure • Depth of Processing • Good Continuation

Dazzle camouflage prevents simple interpretations of boat
type and orientation, making it a difficult target for submarines.

080

Layering

Presenting information in stacked layers to
manage complexity and foster insights.

- Layering is revealing and concealing planes of
  information, one on top of the other, to recontextualize
  information and highlight relationships.

- Opaque layers are useful when additional information
  about a particular item is desired without switching
  contexts (e.g., software pop-up help).

- Transparent layers are useful when overlays of
  information combine to illustrate concepts or highlight
  relationships (e.g., weather maps).

- Consider layering to manage complexity, elaborate
  information, and illustrate concepts without switching
  contexts. Use opaque layers when presenting
  elaborative information. Use transparent layers when
  illustrating concepts or highlighting relationships.

See Also   Hierarchy • Modularity • Progressive Disclosure

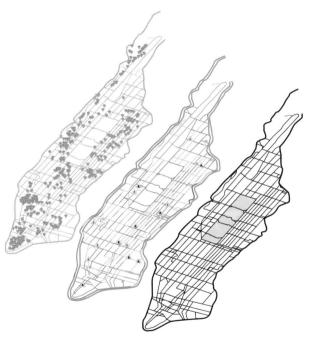

Layering is effectively used in online maps, selectively revealing and concealing useful information like traffic and restaurants.

081

Left-Digit Effect

People overweigh the left-most digits of prices in buying decisions.

- When viewing a price, people have an emotional reaction to the first digit in the sequence and overweigh its value.

- In cultures that read from left to right, this reaction is based on the left-most digit in prices.

- Given two prices, $29.99 and $30.00, people react as if the difference is not one cent, but one dollar. This reaction can increase sales up to 15 percent.

- Prices ending in 99s indicate low prices, but also lower quality. Prices ending in round numbers indicate high prices, but also higher quality.

- Use the left-digit effect when price is more important than quality in buying decisions.

See Also Framing • Priming • Serial Position Effects

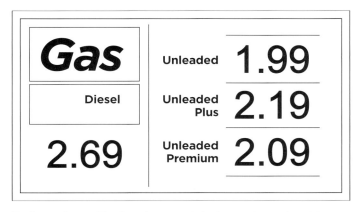

Gas	Unleaded	1.99
Diesel	Unleaded Plus	2.19
2.69	Unleaded Premium	2.09

Ending prices with nines is a good strategy when price drives buying behaviors, as with gasoline.

082

Legibility

The visual clarity of text, generally based on size, typeface, contrast, line length, and spacing.

- Use 9- to 12-point type for high-resolution media such as print. Smaller type is acceptable when limited to captions. Use larger type for low-resolution media.

- Use clear typefaces that can be easily read. There is no performance difference between serif and sans serif typefaces, so select based on aesthetic preference.

- Favor dark text on a light background for optimal legibility. Avoid patterned or textured backgrounds.

- Make line lengths 10–12 words per line, or 35–55 characters per line.

- Set leading (space between text lines, baseline to baseline) to the type size plus 1–4 points. Favor proportionally spaced typefaces to monospaced.

See Also   Chunking • Depth of Processing • Readability

BASELINE

LEADING

BASELINE

ASCENDERS

TYPE SIZE

DESCENDERS

SERIF TYPEFACE
10-POINT TYPE • 12-POINT LEADING • 10 TO 12 WORDS PER LINE

"Oh, I'm not particular as to size," Alice hastily replied;
"only one doesn't like changing so often, you know."

SANS SERIF TYPEFACE
10-POINT TYPE • 12-POINT LEADING • 10 TO 12 WORDS PER LINE

"Oh, I'm not particular as to size," Alice hastily replied;
"only one doesn't like changing so often, you know."

MONOSPACED TYPEFACE
CHARACTERS ARE GIVEN THE SAME AMOUNT OF HORIZONTAL SPACE

The White Rabbit

PROPORTIONALLY SPACED TYPEFACE
CHARACTERS ARE GIVEN DIFFERENT AMOUNTS OF HORIZONTAL SPACE

083

Life Cycle

The common stages of life for products.

- There are four stages of life for products: introduction, growth, maturity, and decline.

- Introduction: The official birth of a product.

- Growth: A stage of rapid expansion. The focus is to scale supply and performance of the product to meet the growing demand, and provide the level of support necessary to maintain customer satisfaction. This is where most products fail.

- Maturity: The peak of the product life cycle. Product sales have begun to diminish, and competition from competitors is strong. The focus is product refinement to maximize customer retention.

- Decline: The end of the life cycle. Product sales continue to decline and core market share is at risk. The focus is to minimize costs and develop transition strategies to migrate customers to new products.

See Also   Development Cycle • Hierarchy of Needs • Iteration

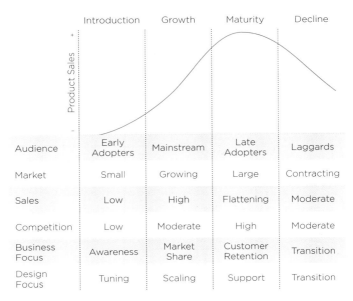

	Introduction	Growth	Maturity	Decline
	Product Sales			
Audience	Early Adopters	Mainstream	Late Adopters	Laggards
Market	Small	Growing	Large	Contracting
Sales	Low	High	Flattening	Moderate
Competition	Low	Moderate	High	Moderate
Business Focus	Awareness	Market Share	Customer Retention	Transition
Design Focus	Tuning	Scaling	Support	Transition

A product needs to evolve over the course of its life to maximize success. Failure to make the right changes at the right time can shorten its life cycle.

084

MAFA Effect

The average face of a local population is generally more attractive than any individual face.

- People find the most average facial appearance (MAFA) of a population more attractive than faces that deviate from the average. Population refers to the group in which a person lives or was raised.

- The effect may be due to the fact that evolution tends to select out extremes. Therefore, a preference for averageness, which results in increased symmetry, may have evolved as an indicator of fitness.

- Use composite images of faces from target populations to represent local perceptions of beauty.

- Consider digital compositing and morphing software to create attractive faces from common faces for advertising and marketing campaigns, especially when real models are unavailable or budgets are limited.

See Also Attractiveness Bias • Baby-Face Bias • Symmetry

2nd
**GENERATION
COMPOSITE**
MAFA

1st GENERATION COMPOSITE

SOURCE

Two generations of composites of four males were sufficient to average out idiosyncratic features and increase symmetry.

085

Magic Triangle

A triangular relationship between facial features that creates the illusion of sentience.

- The magic triangle is a triangular relationship between the eyes, nose, and mouth, developed by Don Sahlin, chief designer of the Muppets.

- In the triangle, pupils are slightly crossed, creating the illusion of focus—like the character is looking at you.

- Smaller pupils make characters look older. Larger pupils make characters look younger.

- Eye placement is considered the most important aspect of the magic triangle. This is the feature that gives life to the character. It is always done last.

- Consider the magic triangle in the design of physical and illustrated characters. Set the eyes last, ensuring a point of focus. Align the size of the eyes and pupils to the age of characters.

See Also   Anthropomorphism • Uncanny Valley

The magic triangle brings character faces to life, creating the illusion of intelligence and self-awareness.

086

Mapping

A correspondence in layout and movement between controls and the things they control.

- Good mapping occurs when there is a strong correspondence in layout and movement between controls and the things they control. Good mapping makes things intuitive to use.

- Bad mapping occurs when there is a weak correspondence in layout and movement between controls and the things they control. Bad mapping makes things counterintuitive to use.

- For example, pushing a switch up to move a car window up is good mapping. Pushing a switch up to move a car window down is bad mapping.

- Ensure good mapping in your designs to minimize errors and make things easy to use.

See Also   Affordance • Constraint • Nudge • Proximity
Similarity • Visibility

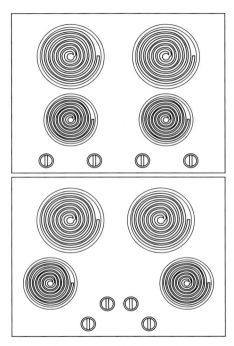

Which stove control turns on which burner? Bad mapping (top) makes it unclear. Good mapping (bottom) makes it intuitive.

087

MAYA

A strategy for determining the most commercially viable aesthetic for a design.

- The most advanced yet acceptable principle (MAYA) was proposed by Raymond Loewy, the father of industrial design.

- MAYA asserts that aesthetic appeal is a balancing act between uniqueness and familiarity—i.e., a product should stretch the definition of a product category, but still be recognizable as a member of that category.

- The principle has been tested empirically, and it does appear that the most novel design that is also somewhat familiar has the greatest aesthetic appeal.

- Consider MAYA when designing for general audiences. In contexts where aesthetic assessments are made by design or art experts, MAYA does not apply. In these cases, novelty is weighed more heavily than familiarity.

See Also   Form Follows Function • IKEA Effect
Mere-Exposure Effect • von Restorff Effect

MAYA explorations by Raymond Loewy demonstrating how the ideal aesthetic form of common products changes over time.

088

Mental Model

A mental simulation of how things work.

- People understand and interact with things by comparing their mental models with the real world. People make errors when their mental models disagree with how things really work.

- Mental models about how things work are called system models. Mental models about how people interact with things are called interaction models.

- Engineers necessarily have strong system models, but typically have weak interaction models. Users develop strong interaction models, but typically have weak system models. Designers must develop strong system and interaction models.

- Leverage existing mental models in design, referencing established conventions and behaviors. Develop strong interaction models by personally using products—i.e., "eating your own dog food"—and observing people using the product.

See Also   Affordance • Expectation Effects • Visibility

CONVENTIONAL BRAKES
on Slick Surfaces

**Pump Brakes and
Do Not Steer**

Noise and vibration are signs
that something is wrong

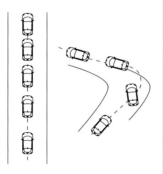

Car will take a longer time to
stop and may make the turn

ABS BRAKES
on Slick Surfaces

**Slam Brakes and
Steer While Braking**

Noise and vibration are signs
that system is operating properly

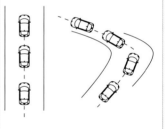

Car will properly stop
and will make the turn

When an interaction model contradicts convention—as with
anti-lock brakes—potential benefits can be slow to materialize.

089

Mere-Exposure Effect

The more people are exposed to a stimulus, the more they like it.

- Repeated exposure to a neutral or positive stimulus makes people like it more. Repeated exposure to a negative stimulus makes people like it less.

- The mere-exposure effect is used in music, slogans, images, advertisements, and political campaigns.

- The mere-exposure effect is strongest during the first 10–20 exposures. Brief exposures are more effective than long exposures.

- Consider the mere-exposure effect to strengthen advertising and marketing campaigns, enhance the credibility and aesthetic of designs, and improve the way people think and feel about a message or product. Keep the exposures brief, and separate them with periods of delay.

See Also Classical Conditioning • Cognitive Dissonance Framing • Priming • Stickiness

The mere-exposure effect is commonly used to increase the likability and support of political leaders. Similar techniques are used in marketing, advertising, and electoral campaigns.

090

Mimicry

Copying properties from familiar things in order to realize benefits of those properties.

- In design, mimicry refers to copying pre-existing solutions to problems. There are three kinds of mimicry: surface, behavioral, and functional.

- Surface Mimicry: copying the way things look (e.g., knock-offs of expensive brands or products).

- Behavioral Mimicry: copying the way things act (e.g., robots simulating human facial expressions).

- Functional Mimicry: copying the way things work (e.g., mimicking the keypad of an adding machine in the design of a touch-tone telephone).

- Mimicry is perhaps the oldest and most efficient method for achieving advances in design. Consider mimicry as one approach in solving problems, considering the surface, behavioral, and functional properties of both natural and man-made things.

See Also   Anthropomorphism • Baby-Face Bias
Savanna Preference • Supernormal Stimulus

Scuba suits that mimic the black and white banding of the Indo-Pacific sea snake show promise as a shark deterrent.

091

Mnemonic Device

A technique for making things easier to remember through patterns of letters or associations.

- Types of mnemonic devices include the following: first-letter, keyword, rhyme, and feature-name.

- First-Letter: The first letter of items to be recalled are used to form the first letters in a meaningful phrase, or combined to form an acronym.

- Keyword: A word that is similar to a word or phrase that is linked to a familiar bridging image.

- Rhyme: One or more words in a phrase are linked to other words through rhyming schemes.

- Feature-Name: A word that is related to one or more features that is linked to a familiar bridging image.

- Use mnemonic devices to increase memorability of logos, slogans, and rote facts. Favor concrete words and images to leverage familiar concepts.

See Also   Recognition Over Recall • Serial Position Effects
Stickiness • von Restorff Effect

Clever use of mnemonic devices can dramatically increase recall, as with this unforgettable dance studio logo.

092

Modularity

Managing system complexity by dividing large
systems into smaller, self-contained systems.

- Modularity involves identifying groups of functions in
  systems, and then transforming those groups into self-
  contained units or modules.

- Modular designs are easier to repair, scale, and
  upgrade, but are significantly more complex to design
  than nonmodular systems.

- Most systems do not begin as modular systems.
  They are incrementally transformed to be modular as
  function sets mature.

- Modular designs encourage innovation. They create
  opportunities for third parties to participate in
  structured design and development.

- Consider modularity when designing complex
  systems. Design modules that conceal their complexity
  and communicate with other modules through simple,
  standard interfaces.

See Also   Cost-Benefit • Flexibility Trade-Offs • Self-Similarity

Google's Project Ara is reinventing the cell phone using modularity. This should reduce costs and open innovation.

093

Normal Distribution

A data set in which many independently measured values of a variable are plotted.

- A normal distribution is a data set in which most of the data are close to the average, and the rest are equally distributed on either side of the average. The result is a symmetrical bell-shaped curve.

- Normal distributions are found everywhere—annual temperature averages, stock market fluctuations, student test scores—and are thus commonly used to determine the parameters of a design.

- Do not design for the average person. For example, a shoe designed for the average foot size would fit only about 68 percent of the population.

- Aspire to create designs that accommodate 98 percent of a population. While it is sometimes possible to design for everyone, this generally results in diminishing returns.

See Also Convergence • MAFA Effect • MAYA • Selection Bias

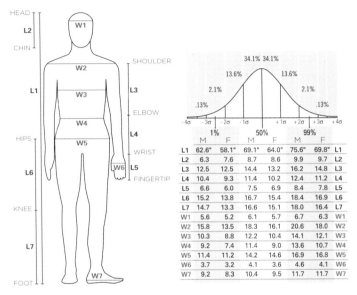

	1% M	1% F	50% M	50% F	99% M	99% F	
L1	62.6"	58.1"	69.1"	64.0"	75.6"	69.8"	L1
L2	6.3	7.6	8.7	8.6	9.9	9.7	L2
L3	12.5	12.5	14.4	13.2	16.2	14.8	L3
L4	10.4	9.3	11.4	10.2	12.4	11.2	L4
L5	6.6	6.0	7.5	6.9	8.4	7.8	L5
L6	15.2	13.8	16.7	15.4	18.4	16.9	L6
L7	14.7	13.3	16.6	15.1	18.0	16.4	L7
W1	5.6	5.2	6.1	5.7	6.7	6.3	W1
W2	15.8	13.5	18.3	16.1	20.6	18.0	W2
W3	10.3	8.8	12.2	10.4	14.1	12.1	W3
W4	9.2	7.4	11.4	9.0	13.6	10.7	W4
W5	11.4	11.2	14.2	14.6	16.9	16.8	W5
W6	3.7	3.2	4.1	3.6	4.6	4.1	W6
W7	9.2	8.3	10.4	9.5	11.7	11.7	W7

The measures of men and women are normally distributed. The wide range of measures across the distribution illustrates the problem of simply designing for an average person.

094

Not Invented Here

A tendency to oppose ideas and innovations that originate outside of your social group.

- The not-invented-here bias (NIH) is an organizational phenomenon in which groups resist ideas and contributions from external sources, often resulting in "reinventing the wheel".

- Four social dynamics appear to underlie NIH: belief that internal capabilities are superior to external capabilities, fear of losing control, desire for credit and status, and significant emotional and financial investment in internal initiatives.

- The primary ways to overcome NIH are educating the organization about the bias, encouraging collaboration with outsiders, and increasing familiarity with products from partners and competitors.

- Raise awareness of NIH and its underlying social dynamics in your organization. Recognition is the first step to both recovery and prevention.

See Also   Cognitive Dissonance • Design by Committee

In 1982, Timex licensed the Sinclair ZX-81 for resale in the U.S. Sales were strong. The not-invented-here bias led Timex to make hardware changes, which created software compatibility problems. Timex dropped out of the computer market in 1984.

095

Nudge

A method of modifying behavior without restricting options or changing incentives.

- Nudges use the following methods to modify behavior: smart defaults, clear feedback, aligned incentives, structured choices, and visible goals.

- Smart Defaults: Select defaults that do the least harm and most good versus the most conservative defaults.

- Clear Feedback: Provide clear, visible, and immediate feedback for actions.

- Aligned Incentives: Align incentives to preferred behaviors, avoiding incentive conflicts.

- Structured Choices: Provide the means to simplify and filter complexity to facilitate decision making.

- Visible Goals: Make simple performance measures clearly visible so that people can immediately assess their performance against goals.

See Also Constraint • Framing • Gamification • Hick's Law

Why does etching an image of a fly into urinals reduce spillage by 80 percent? When people see a target, they try to hit it.

096

Ockham's Razor

Simple designs should be preferred.

- Named after William of Ockham, a fourteenth-century Franciscan friar and logician who reputedly made abundant use of the principle.

- Given two functionally equivalent designs, the simpler design should be preferred.

- Applying Ockham's razor means cutting unnecessary elements from a design.

- Proficient designers favor simplicity over ornamentation, supporting use of Ockham's razor.

- Apply Ockham's razor to elements in your design. If the design is no worse for their loss, apply it again.

See Also   Form Follows Function • Horror Vacui • KISS Mapping • Signal-to-Noise Ratio

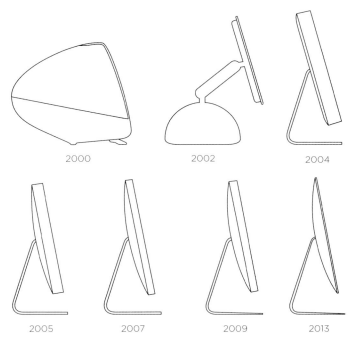

2000

2002

2004

2005

2007

2009

2013

The evolution of the iMac proves that no company wields Ockham's razor with the skill and aggression of Apple.

097

Operant Conditioning

Using rewards and punishments to modify behavior.

- A technique used to increase behavior by following it with rewards, or decrease behavior by following it with punishment. Rewards and punishments are most effective when administered right after a behavior.

- Commonly used in animal training, behavior modification, and incentive systems.

- Over-rewarding can undermine intrinsic motivation. For example, lavishly rewarding people to perform tasks they enjoy will diminish their enjoyment of those tasks.

- Predictable reward schedules result in low performance that extinguishes quickly if the rewards stop. Less predictable reward schedules result in high performance that is resistant to extinction if rewards stop.

- Consider operant conditioning to change behaviors. Avoid over-rewarding behaviors when intrinsic motivation exists. Favor unpredictable over predictable reward schedules for peak performance.

See Also   Classical Conditioning • Gamification • Shaping

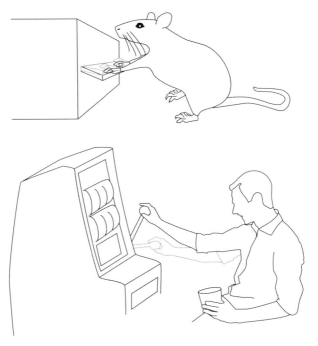

Whether a lever-pressing rat or a slot-playing human, rewards delivered right after the behavior make it addictive by design.

098

Orientation Sensitivity

Certain line orientations are more quickly and easily processed and discriminated than others.

- People can accurately judge vertical and horizontal lines, but have problems judging diagonal lines.

- Lines differing in orientation by more than 30 degrees from a background of lines are easy to detect, and differing by less than 30 degrees difficult to detect.

- Compositions where the primary elements have vertical or horizontal orientations are considered more aesthetic than diagonal orientations.

- Consider orientation sensitivity in compositions requiring discrimination between lines. Facilitate discrimination between lines by making their orientation differ by more than 30 degrees. Use horizontal and vertical lines as visual anchors to enhance aesthetics and maximize discrimination.

See Also   Alignment • Figure-Ground • Good Continuation
Highlighting • Signal-to-Noise Ratio

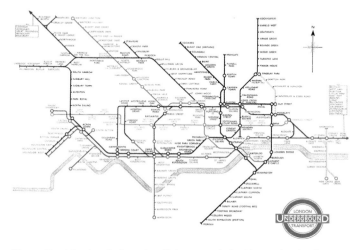

Harry Beck's classic London Tube map is both aesthetically pleasing and easy to read because railway lines are only represented in vertical, horizontal, and 45-degree orientations.

099

Performance Load

The mental and physical effort required to
complete a task.

- There are two types of performance load: cognitive
  and kinematic.

- Cognitive load is the mental effort required to
  accomplish a goal (e.g., recalling a new phone
  number). Kinematic load is the physical effort required
  to accomplish a goal (e.g., dialing a phone number).

- When performance load is high, time and errors
  increase. When performance load is low, time and
  errors decrease.

- Minimize cognitive load by reducing information
  density, reducing the mental effort required to
  perform tasks, and automating tasks when possible.

- Minimize kinematic load by reducing the number of
  steps in tasks, reducing the physical effort required to
  perform tasks, and automating tasks when possible.

See Also   Accessibility • Cost-Benefit • Depth of Processing

Classic photo from a time-motion study conducted by Frank and Lillian Gilbreth to reduce time and effort to perform tasks.

100

Performance vs. Preference

Increasing performance does not necessarily increase desirability.

- People often believe that a functionally superior design—the proverbial "better mousetrap"—is good design. This is not necessarily correct.

- The reasons people favor one design over another is a combination of many factors, and may have nothing to do with performance, but with preference.

- Preferences may be based on innate tendencies, cultural biases, aesthetic or emotional considerations, or legacy practices and conventions.

- Success in design is multivariate. Consider both performance and preference factors in design to maximize the probability of success. Beware the trap of creating a superior product in one dimension, but having it fail due to neglect of other dimensions.

See Also   Aesthetic-Usability Effect • Control • Desire Lines
Flexibility Trade-Offs • Hierarchy of Needs

QWERTY Keyboard

Dvorak Keyboard

The performance advantages of the Dvorak keyboard are no match for the generations of users trained on QWERTY.

101

Phonetic Symbolism

The meaning conveyed by the sounds of words.

- Certain letter sounds symbolize size, gender, and aggression, and reinforce these meanings in words.

- Consonant sounds with a constant flow of air—such as the letters *s*, *f*, *v*, *z*—are associated with smallness, femininity, and passivity. Consonant sounds where the air is blocked—like the letters *p*, *k*, *t*, *b*, *g*, *d*, hard *c*—are associated with largeness, masculinity, and aggression.

- Vowel sounds that widen the mouth, as with a smile— *e* (bee), *i* (sit), *a* (hate), *e* (best)—are associated with smallness, femininity, and passivity. Vowel sounds that bring the mouth into a circle—*o* (dome), *o* (caught), *a* (can), *u* (food), *u* (put), *u* (luck), *a* (cot)—are associated with largeness, masculinity, and aggression.

- Consider phonetic symbolism in naming and pricing. Ensure that the phonetic symbolism of brands and important numbers are congruent with their meanings.

See Also   Affordance • Priming • Propositional Density

Mhysa

{Mee-Sah}

noun. Mother

Dracarys

{Dra-KAH-ris}

noun. Dragon Fire

Phonetic symbolism makes these terms from *Game of Thrones* somewhat intelligible even though the languages are fictional.

102

Picture Superiority Effect

Pictures are remembered better than words.

- Pictures are better recognized and recalled than words, although memory for pictures and words together is superior to either one alone.

- When recall is measured immediately after the presentation of pictures or words, recall for both is equal. When recall is measured more than thirty seconds after presentation, pictures are recalled significantly better.

- The recall advantage increases when exposure is casual and time-limited. For example, walking by an advertisement with a picture is more likely to be recalled than an advertisement without a picture.

- Use the picture superiority effect to improve recognition and recall. Use pictures and words together when possible, ensuring that they reinforce one another for optimal effect.

See Also Iconic Representation • Inattentional Blindness
Mere-Exposure Effect • Recognition Over Recall

The authors know you are looking at the pictures in this book first, and then begrudgingly reading the text when needed.

103

Priming

Activating specific concepts in memory to
influence subsequent thoughts and behaviors.

- Priming is the intentional activation of specific
  memories in an audience for the purposes of influence.

- When we perceive the outside world, associated
  memories are automatically activated. Once activated,
  these memories can influence subsequent thoughts,
  emotions, and behaviors.

- Priming will not induce people to act against their
  values, but it can increase the probability of people of
  engaging in behaviors consistent with their values.

- Consider priming in all aspects of design. First
  impressions and antecedent events are opportunities
  to influence subsequent reactions and behaviors.

See Also   Expectation Effects • Framing • Nudge
             Red Effects • Serial-Position Effects

A poster that primes being watched versus a generic poster can significantly reduce malfeasant behavior.

104

Progressive Disclosure

A method of managing complexity, in which only necessary or requested information is displayed.

- Progressive disclosure is used to prevent information overload and provide step-by-step guidance. It involves separating information into layers, and only presenting layers that are necessary or relevant.

- Progressive disclosure is used in user interfaces, instructional materials, and the design of physical spaces. It can also be applied to differentially support users of different skill levels; for example, displaying advanced features to advanced users only.

- Use progressive disclosure to reduce information complexity. Consider hiding infrequently used controls or information, but make them available through simple requests, such as pressing a "More" button. When procedures are sensitive to error, use progressive disclosure to lead novices through the procedure step by step.

See Also   Control • Errors • Layering • Performance Load

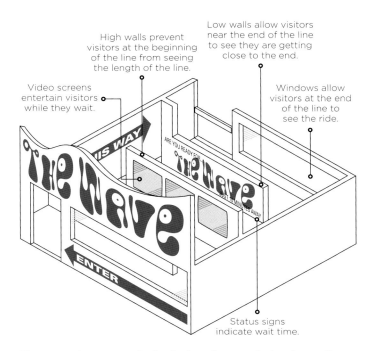

Video screens entertain visitors while they wait.

High walls prevent visitors at the beginning of the line from seeing the length of the line.

Low walls allow visitors near the end of the line to see they are getting close to the end.

Windows allow visitors at the end of the line to see the ride.

Status signs indicate wait time.

THE WAVE

THIS WAY

ENTER

ARE YOU READY FOR

THE WAVE

JUST 17 MINUTES AWAY

Theme parks progressively disclose lines so that only small segments of the line can be seen from any particular point.

105

Propositional Density

The relationship between the elements of a design and the meanings they convey.

- A proposition is a simple statement about a thing that cannot be made simpler. Propositional density is the amount of information conveyed per unit element.

- There are two types of propositions: surface and deep. Surface propositions are visible elements. Deep propositions are the meanings they convey.

- Propositional density can be estimated by dividing the number of deep propositions by the number of surface propositions. A propositional density greater than one makes things engaging and memorable.

- Strive to achieve the highest propositional density possible, but make sure the deep propositions are complementary. Contradictory deep propositions confuse the message and nullify the benefits.

See Also   Framing • Inverted Pyramid • Stickiness

Barack Obama's 2008 campaign logo has a high propositional density, a key to its success. There are three visible elements (e.g., blue circle), and approximately ten meanings (e.g., O for Obama, American flag, etc.). PD = 10 / 3 = 3.33.

106

Prospect-Refuge

A preference for environments with unobstructed views, areas of concealment, and paths of retreat.

- The design goal of prospect-refuge is to create spaces where people can see without being seen.

- People prefer the edges versus middles of spaces, ceilings or covers overhead, spaces with few access points, and spaces that provide unobstructed views from multiple vantage points.

- Consider prospect-refuge in the creation of landscapes, residences, offices, and communities.

- Create multiple vantage points within a space, so that the internal and external areas can be easily surveyed.

- Make large, open areas more appealing by using screening elements to create partial refuges.

See Also   Biophilia Effect • Cathedral Effect
Defensible Space • Savanna Preference

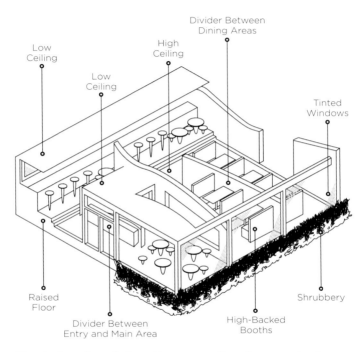

Low
Ceiling

Low
Ceiling

High
Ceiling

Divider Between
Dining Areas

Tinted
Windows

Raised
Floor

Divider Between
Entry and Main Area

High-Backed
Booths

Shrubbery

The design of a cafe from the perspective of prospect-refuge.

107

Prototyping

Rapidly building low-fidelity models to explore ideas and deeply understand problems.

- Prototyping is research, not development. The goal of prototyping is understanding.

- Iterative prototyping—i.e., rapidly building a series of prototypes to find solutions to problems—is the basis of "design thinking".

- Prototypes should use simple software tools or readily available materials and makeshift fabrication to accelerate construction. The rate of prototyping is effectively the rate of learning.

- Discard prototypes once they serve their purpose. Prototypes should generally not become products.

- Use prototyping to understand problems deeply and explore solutions quickly. Prototype to the level of understanding: build basic prototypes when understanding is basic, and build increasingly advanced prototypes as understanding develops.

See Also Iteration • KISS • Satisficing • Scaling Fallacy

Problem-solving challenges involving many unknowns and time constraints are best solved through rapid prototyping.

108

Proximity

Things that are close together are perceived to be more related than things that are farther apart.

- One of the Gestalt principles of perception.

- Proximity is one of the most powerful means of indicating relatedness in design, and will generally overwhelm competing visual cues.

- Degrees of proximity imply degrees of relatedness.

- Certain proximal layouts imply specific kinds of relationships. For example, touching or overlapping elements are interpreted as sharing one or more attributes; whereas proximal but nontouching elements are interpreted as related but independent.

- Arrange elements so that proximity corresponds to relatedness. Ensure that labels and supporting information are near the elements they describe. Favor direct labeling over legends or keys.

See Also Common Fate • Figure-Ground • Good Continuation
Law of Prägnanz • Uniform Connectedness

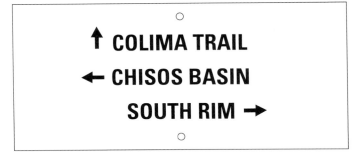

This sign at Big Bend (top) misleads hikers by using proximity incorrectly. The redesign (bottom) fixes the problem.

109

Readability

The ease with which text can be understood,
based on the complexity of words and sentences.

- Readability is one of the most overlooked and
  important aspects of design.

- Readability is determined by factors such as word
  length, word commonality, sentence length, clauses
  per sentence, and syllables per sentence.

- Readability can be improved by omitting needless
  words and punctuation, avoiding acronyms and jargon,
  keeping sentence length appropriate for the intended
  audience, and using active voice.

- When targeting a specific reading level, consider
  readability formulas designed for this purpose.

- Consider readability when creating designs that
  involve narrative text. Ensure that the reading level
  is audience appropriate. Strive to express complex
  concepts in simple ways, using plain language.

See Also Inverted Pyramid • KISS • Stickiness • Storytelling

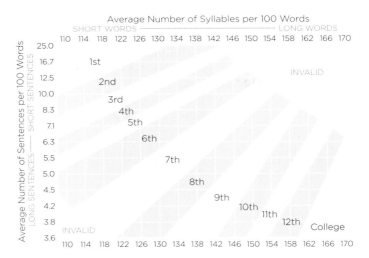

Fry's Readability Graph is one of many tools that can be used to ensure that readability of text is audience appropriate.

110

Reciprocity

The tendency for people to give back to those who have given to them.

- Reciprocity is a tendency to respond to kindness with kindness. Anything that is perceived as a gift or concession creates the effect.

- The acts that create reciprocity most effectively are meaningful, personalized, and unexpected. Reciprocity only works if the initiating act is perceived as sincere.

- For example, a nonprofit organization sending mail-outs that contain useful, personalized gifts—such as mailing labels—will receive significantly more donations in greater amounts than sending just a solicitation letter.

- Use reciprocity to promote goodwill, garner attention and consideration, and move people to action. Apply the principle sincerely and sparingly, else it will be perceived as manipulative.

See Also Framing • IKEA Effect • Nudge • Scarcity • Shaping

After a decade of mailing out free-trial CDs, AOL increased its subscribership 12,000 percent. The campaign used reciprocity effectively in the early stages, but they didn't know when to stop. As people began receiving multiple CDs, the once novel gesture looked increasingly like a wasteful manipulation.

111

Recognition Over Recall

Memory for recognizing things is better than memory for recalling things.

- Recognition is easier than recall because recognition tasks provide cues that facilitate a memory search.

- The principle is often used in interface design. For example, early computers used command line interfaces, which required recall memory for hundreds of commands. Modern computers use graphical user interfaces with commands in menus, which only require recognition of desired commands.

- Decision making is also influenced by recognition. Familiar options are selected over unfamiliar options, even when the unfamiliar option may be the best choice. Recognition of an option is often a sufficient condition for making a choice.

- Minimize the need for recall whenever possible. Use menus, decision aids, and similar strategies to make available options clear and visible.

See Also   Mere-Exposure Effect • Performance Load • Visibility

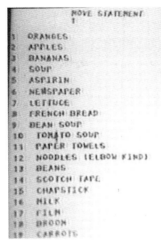

On December 9, 1968, Douglas Engelbart gave "The Mother of All Demos", which laid the foundation for user interfaces based on recognition over recall. This not only made computers easier to use, it enabled them to become mass-market products.

112

Red Effects

A set of cognitive and behavioral effects triggered by exposure to the color red.

- Red makes women appear more sexual.

- Red makes men appear more dominant.

- Wearing red apparel confers a small competitive advantage in sports contests.

- Red increases performance on simple physical tasks, but impairs problem solving and creativity.

- Red promotes competitive behaviors, but undermines cooperative behaviors.

- Use red to increase general attractiveness, gain an edge in competitive contexts, and increase competitive behaviors. Avoid red in environments requiring learning, testing, and cooperation.

See Also Attractiveness Bias • Blue Effects • Priming

A lady in red exaggerates her fertility, making her more sexually attractive to males.

113

Redundancy

Using back-up or fail-safe elements to maintain system performance in the event of failure.

• Redundancy is the most reliable method of preventing catastrophic failure.

• When the causes of failure cannot be anticipated, use different kinds of redundancy; for example, having both a hydraulic and a mechanical brake.

• When the causes of failure can be anticipated, use more of the same kinds of redundancy; for example, using independent strands of fiber to weave a rope.

• When performance interruptions are not tolerable, make redundant elements active at all times; for example, using additional columns to support a roof.

• When performance interruptions are tolerable, make redundant elements passive but available; for example, having a spare tire in the event of a flat tire.

See Also   Crowd Intelligence • Factor of Safety • Modularity
Saint-Venant's Principle • Weakest Link

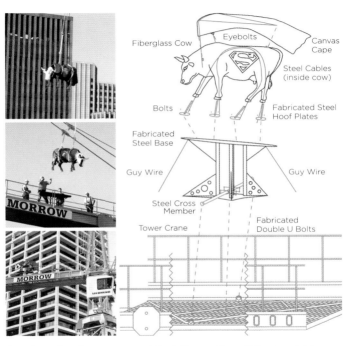

Labels on diagram:

Fiberglass Cow — Eyebolts — Canvas Cape

Steel Cables (inside cow)

Bolts — Fabricated Steel Hoof Plates

Fabricated Steel Base

Guy Wire — Guy Wire

Steel Cross Member

Tower Crane — Fabricated Double U Bolts

MORROW

Ample redundancy ensured that Super Cow did not get blown off of his thirty-story perch during hurricane season.

114

Root Cause

The key initiating cause in a sequence of events that leads to an event of interest.

- Most problems, especially difficult problems, have multiple causes, and their proximal causes are rarely their root causes. The root cause is the key event in a cause-event sequence that leads to a problem.

- Asking "why?" an event occurred five times (plus or minus) is an effective way to identify root causes.

- For example: Why did the welder burn herself? She wasn't wearing protective clothing. Why wasn't she wearing protective clothing? It was hot in the room. Why was it so hot? The air conditioner was broken. The root cause of the accident was a broken AC.

- Focus on root causes when troubleshooting problems. Use the *five whys* technique to identify root causes and other elements in the causal chain. Since asking why can lead to infinite regress, focus on actionable causes that create the majority of the effects.

See Also 80/20 Rule • Confirmation Bias • Errors • Visibility

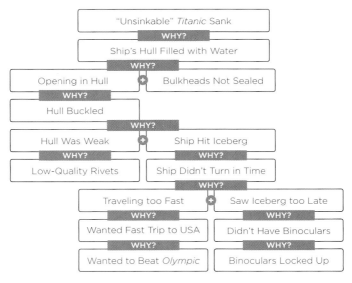

A partial cause map exploring root causes for the sinking of the RMS *Titanic*. It is oversimple to blame the iceberg.

115 Rosetta Stone

A strategy for communicating novel information using elements of common understanding.

- The Rosetta Stone is an Egyptian artifact inscribed with one message in three scripts. Modern knowledge of one of the scripts enabled scholars to translate the other two unknown scripts.

- Applying the Rosetta Stone principle involves embedding elements of common understanding in messages, called keys, to act as bridging elements from the known to the unknown.

- Make it clear that keys are keys, to be interpreted first and used as a point of reference.

- Deliver messages in stages, with each stage acting as a supporting key for subsequent stages.

- When you don't know what level of understanding the recipient will have, embed multiple keys based on widely understood or universal concepts.

See Also   Archetypes • Comparison • Iconic Representation
Propositional Density • Uniform Connectedness

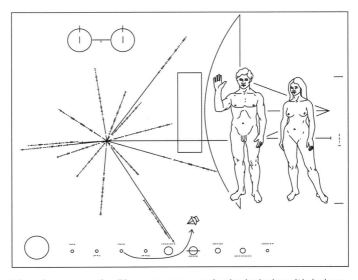

The plaques on the Pioneer space probe included multiple keys to help ETs decipher its message, including representations of hydrogen, the relative position of the Sun to the center of the Galaxy and fourteen pulsars, and silhouettes of the spacecraft.

116

Rule of Thirds

A technique of composition in which a medium is divided into thirds.

- The rule of thirds is derived from the use of early grid systems in composition.

- Application of the rule of thirds generally results in aesthetically pleasing compositions.

- Divide a medium into thirds, both vertically and horizontally, creating an invisible grid of nine rectangles and four intersections.

- Position key elements at the points of intersection on the grid, vertical elements to vertical lines, and horizontal elements to horizontal lines.

- Do not use the rule of thirds when a composition is symmetrical and contains one dominant element. Centering in this case will increase dramatic effect.

See Also   Alignment • Area Alignment • Golden Ratio
Symmetry • Wabi-Sabi

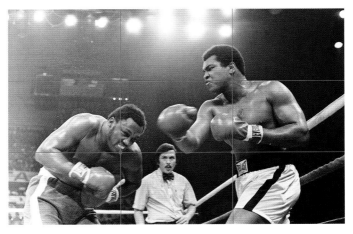

This photo from the "Thrilla in Manila" makes excellent use of the rule of thirds, placing the heads of both fighters at opposing intersections on the grid.

117

Saint-Venant's Principle

Local effects of loads on structures have negligible global effects.

- Proposed by French mathematician and engineer Adhémar Barré de Saint-Venant.

- Load effects at one point of concentration on a structure become negligible a short distance away from that point. For example, overtightening a bolt deforms just the region that is near the hole.

- Locate loads closer than 3–5 characteristic lengths to merge load effects. For example, spacing bolts less than 3–5 bolt diameters apart creates a weld-like join. Separate loads more than 3–5 characteristic lengths to keep load effects isolated.

- Secure structural and mechanical systems by controlling 3–5 characteristic aspects of a system. For example, the anchored section of a cantilevered arm should be 3–5 times the length of the cantilever.

See Also Factor of Safety • Redundancy • Satisficing

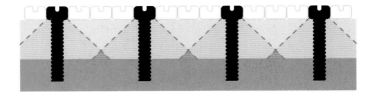

Bolts spaced within 3-5 bolt diameters apart (top) have overlapping stress cones, forming a weld-like connection. Bolts spaced farther apart (bottom) have negligible impact on one another. Both effects are due to Saint-Venant's principle.

118

Satisficing

A problem solving strategy that seeks a satisfactory versus optimal solution.

- In certain circumstances, seeking to roughly satisfy—i.e., satisfice—design requirements is more productive than seeking to optimally satisfy design requirements.

- When problems are complex or time-constrained, satisficing is more productive than optimizing.

- Satisficing is the basis for iterative prototyping, design thinking, and most real-world problem solving. It epitomizes the maxim: "Don't let perfect be the enemy of good."

- Use satisficing versus optimizing when problems are complex or time-limited—in other words, for most problems most of the time. Once a problem is solved, the solution can be optimized as time permits.

See Also 80/20 Rule • Cost-Benefit • Iteration • KISS
Prototyping • Root Cause

The legendary makeshift adapter that fit a square CO_2 filter to a round receptacle on Apollo 13. NASA satisficing perfection.

119

Savanna Preference

A preference for savannalike environments over other types of environments.

- Humans prefer parklike landscapes that feature openness, uniform grass, scattered trees, visible water, and signs of wildlife.

- The savanna preference likely provided adaptive benefits to human ancestors—i.e., those who lived in savannas enjoyed a survival advantage over those who lived in harsher environments.

- The savanna preference is found across all age ranges and cultures, but it is strongest in children.

- Consider the savanna preference when featuring landscapes in art, advertising, and other contexts involving depictions of natural environments—especially contexts involving young children, such as stories, toys, and play environments.

See Also Archetypes • Biophilia Effect • Defensible Space
Prospect-Refuge • Self-Similarity

The Teletubbies mesmerized children in more than sixty countries and thirty-five languages. Simple stories, baby-faced creatures, and a savanna landscape equal excellent design for young children.

120

Scaling Fallacy

Designs that work at one scale often do not work at smaller or larger scales.

- Designs often perform differently at different scales because the forces involved scale in different ways. Two types of scaling assumptions result in scaling errors: load and interaction.

- Load assumptions are assumptions that working stresses will be the same when a design changes scale.

- Interaction assumptions are assumptions that the way people and other systems interact with a design will be the same when a design changes scale.

- Minimize scaling assumptions in design by raising awareness, testing assumptions, and researching analogous designs. When you are unable to verify scaling effects, build in factors of safety.

See Also Factor of Safety • Feedback Loop • Modularity
Prototyping • Redundancy • Satisficing

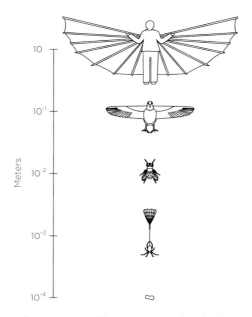

Flapping to fly works at mid-range scales, but it does not work at very small scales where wings can't displace air molecules, or at large scales where the effects of gravity are too great.

121

Scarcity

Things become more desirable when they are in short supply or occur infrequently.

- Scarce items are more valued than plentiful items.
- Scarcity motivates people to act.
- Apply the principle through: exclusivity, limited access, limited time, limited number, and surprise.
- The principle holds across the spectrum of human behavior, from mate attraction to marketing to tactics of negotiation.
- The effect is strongest when the desired object or opportunity is highly unique, and not easily obtained or approximated by other means.
- Consider scarcity when designing advertising and promotional initiatives, especially when the objective is to move people to action.

See Also Expectation Effect • Framing • Veblen Effect

The *Running of the Brides* event at Filene's Basement offers bargain-basement prices on bridal gowns once a year, one day only. The competitive shopping chaos that ensues is a case study in the power of scarcity.

122

Selection Bias

A bias in the way evidence is collected that distorts analysis and conclusions.

- Selection bias results from the non-random sampling of evidence. Accordingly, it over-represents certain aspects of the evidence and under-represents others, distorting analysis and conclusions.

- For example, if subscribers of a science magazine are surveyed and their responses generalized to the overall population, science-minded viewpoints would be over-represented in the analysis and results.

- Avoid selection bias. Collect data from entire populations when they are small. Randomly sample from populations when they are large.

- Scrutinize the selected population and sampling methods when evaluating conclusions based on statistical analysis.

See Also   Confirmation Bias • Garbage In-Garbage Out
Normal Distribution • Uncertainty Principle

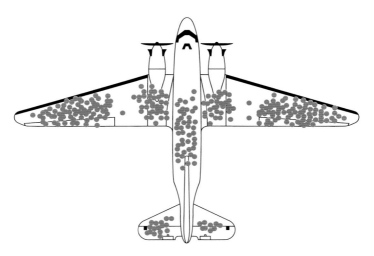

The red dots indicate areas of combat damage received by surviving WWII bombers. Where would you add armor to increase survivability? The statistician Abraham Wald recommended reinforcing the areas *without* damage. Since these data came from surviving aircraft only, bombers hit in undotted areas were the ones that did not make it back.

123

Self-Similarity

A property in which a thing is composed of similar patterns at multiple levels of scale.

- Natural forms exhibit similarity at multiple scales. Accordingly, self-similarity is often considered a universal aesthetic.

- People find self-similar forms beautiful, especially when the mathematical density of the pattern resembles savanna-like environments and trees.

- Self-similar modularity is an effective means of scaling systems and managing complexity.

- Explore self-similarity in all aspects of design: storytelling, music composition, visual displays, and engineering. Use it to enhance aesthetics, manage complexity, and scale systems.

See Also   Archetypes • Hierarchy • Modularity
Savanna Preference • Similarity • Symmetry

The Mona Lisa photomosaic, the African acacia tree, fractals, and Roman aqueducts all exhibit self-similarity.

124

Serial Position Effects

Things presented at the beginning and end of a sequence are more memorable than things presented in the middle.

- Things presented first generally have the greatest influence; they are not only better recalled, but influence the interpretation of later items. For example, words presented early in sentences have more impact than words presented later.

- Things presented last are more memorable when the presentations are separated in time, and a person is recalling information or making a selection soon after the last presentation.

- Use serial position effects to increase recall or influence the selection of specific items. Present important items at the beginning or end of a sequence in order to maximize recall.

See Also Chunking • Interference Effects • Left-Digit Effect

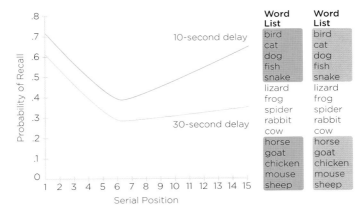

Items at the beginning and end of lists are easier to remember than items in the middle. If recall is attempted 10 seconds after the list is presented (RED), recall is about the same. If recall is attempted more than 30 seconds after the list is presented (BLUE), the items at the beginning are still easily recalled, whereas the items at the end are becoming less memorable.

125

Shaping

Training a target behavior by reinforcing successive approximations of that behavior.

- First studied by the psychologist B.F. Skinner, a pioneer in behavior modification.

- Shaping involves breaking down a complex behavior into a chain of simple behaviors, which are trained one by one until the complex behavior is achieved.

- Positive reinforcement is provided as an observed behavior increasingly approximates a target behavior.

- Shaping results in the development of superstitious behaviors when irrelevant behaviors are accidentally reinforced during training.

- Use shaping to train complex behaviors in games and learning environments, teach rote procedures, and refine complex motor tasks.

See Also Classical Conditioning • Operant Conditioning

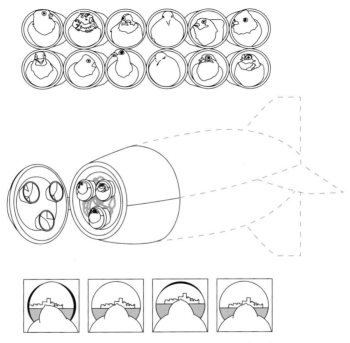

During WWII, B.F. Skinner used shaping to train pigeons to peck at aerial photographs, creating pigeon-guided bombs.

126

Signal-to-Noise Ratio

The ratio of relevant to irrelevant information.
Good designs have high signal-to-noise ratios.

• In communication, the form of the information—*the signal*—is sometimes degraded, and extraneous information—*the noise*—is added.

• Signal degradation occurs when information is presented inefficiently: unclear writing, inappropriate graphs, unnecessary elements, or ambiguous icons.

• Signal strength occurs when information is presented simply and concisely, using redundant coding, and highlighting of important elements.

• Maximize signal-to-noise ratio in design. Increase signal by keeping designs simple. Consider enhancing key aspects of information through techniques like redundant coding and highlighting. Minimize noise by removing unnecessary elements, and minimizing the expression of elements.

See Also   KISS • Ockham's Razor • Performance Load

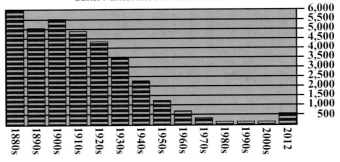

Babies Named Alice Per Million Babies

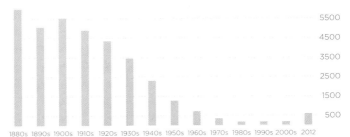

Babies Named Alice Per Million Babies

Reduce noise in graphs by removing unnecessary elements and quieting the expression of necessary elements.

127

Similarity

Things that are similar are perceived to be more related than things that are dissimilar.

- One of the Gestalt principles of perception.

- Similarity indicates and reinforces the relatedness of elements. Lack of similarity indicates and reinforces differences among elements.

- Color similarity is an effective grouping strategy when there are no more than 3-4 colors, and the design is still usable by the color blind. Size and shape similarity are effective grouping strategies when elements are clearly distinguishable from one another.

- Design elements so that similarity corresponds to relatedness. Design unrelated- or ambiguously-related items using different colors, sizes, and shapes.

- Use the fewest colors and simplest shapes possible for the strongest grouping effects, ensuring that elements are sufficiently distinct to be detectable.

See Also   Chunking • Consistency • Mimicry • Self-Similarity

The Tivo remote control uses buttons of different colors, sizes, and shapes to reduce complexity and improve usability.

128

Social Trap

A tendency to pursue short-term gains that create long-term losses for the greater group.

- A situation in which people act to obtain short-term gains, and in so doing create losses for everyone in their group, including themselves.

- For example, ranchers overgraze cattle on public land. This depletes the land of grasses faster than the land can replenish. This then starves all of the ranchers' cattle, including the original overgrazers.

- Social traps are most problematic when a resource is readily available and highly desirable, when people compete to access and use that resource, and when the long-term costs are not visible or easily monitored.

- Mitigate the effects of social traps by enforcing sustainable limits on resource use (e.g., fishing limits), rewarding cooperation and punishing freeloading, and increasing the visibility of long-term costs.

See Also Confirmation Bias • Gamification • Nudge
Sunk Cost Effect • Uncertainty Principle • Visibility

Despite everyone wanting to get home as fast as possible, traffic jams occur—but rarely on tollways. Having to pay tolls to drive on the roads moderates use, mitigating the social trap.

129

Stickiness

A formula for increasing the recognition, recall, and voluntary sharing of an idea.

- Stickiness explains why certain ideas go viral and become lodged in the cultural consciousness. It is characterized by the following six attributes, which form the mnemonic *SUCCES*:

  1. Simple: Sticky ideas can be expressed simply and succinctly without sacrificing depth.

  2. Unexpected: Sticky ideas contain an element of surprise, which grabs attention.

  3. Concrete: Sticky ideas are specific and concrete, typically using plain language or imagery.

  4. Credible: Sticky ideas are believable, often communicated by a trusted source.

  5. Emotional: Sticky ideas elicit an emotional reaction.

  6. Stories: Sticky ideas are expressible as stories, increasing their memorability and retelling.

See Also   Inverted Pyramid • Storytelling • von Restorff Effect

From WWII British motivational poster to modern-day meme, the enduring popularity of the message owes to its stickiness.

130

Storytelling

Evoking imagery, emotions, and understanding through the presentation of events.

- Storytelling is the original method of passing knowledge from one generation to the next.

- Good storytelling requires certain fundamental elements, including a setting (e.g., time and place), characters with whom the audience can identify, a plot that ties events together, events and atmospherics that evoke emotions, and a pace and flow that maintains the audience's interest.

- Good storytelling minimizes the storyteller.

- Good stories tend to follow archetypal plots.

- Use storytelling to engage audiences, evoke emotions, and enhance learning. When successful, an audience will experience and recall the events of the story in a personal way. It becomes a part of them.

See Also   Archetypes • Stickiness • Zeigarnik Effect

Southern Poverty
Law Center in
Montgomery, AL
SETTING

Timeline
of Events
PLOT

Civil Rights
Activists
CHARACTERS

Reflective Stone,
Falling Water
MOOD

The Civil Rights Memorial tells the story of the civil rights movement using all of the fundamental storytelling elements.

131

Structural Forms

There are three structural strategies for creating things: mass, frames, and shells.

- Mass structures consist of materials that are piled or stacked to create solid forms. Their strength is a function of the weight and hardness of the materials. Consider mass structures for barriers and small shelters, especially when building materials are limited.

- Frame structures consist of struts joined to form a skeleton. Their strength is a function of the strength of the elements and joints, and their organization. Consider frames for large structures.

- Shell structures consist of materials that wrap around to contain a volume. They maintain their form and support loads without a frame or solid mass inside. Their strength is a function of their ability to distribute loads throughout the structure. Consider shell structures for containers, small cast structures, shelters, and designs requiring large spans.

See Also Factor of Safety • Modularity • Scaling Fallacy

Frames work well for large structures. Shells work well for lightweight shelters. Mass forms work well for simple barriers.

132

Sunk Cost Effect

The tendency to continue investing in an endeavor because of past investments in that endeavor.

- People frequently let past investments influence future investments. For example, you buy a nonrefundable ticket to a show, decide you no longer want to go to the show, but you go anyway because you paid for it.

- Rationally speaking, past investments, or sunk costs, should not influence decision making. Only the cost-benefits of current options should influence decisions.

- People are susceptible to the effect because they fear losses more than they desire gains, and because they do not want to feel or appear wasteful. The effect leads people and organizations to make bad decisions, throwing good money after bad.

- Recognizing the sunk cost effect is the first step to recovery. Focus on current cost-benefits only. Beware the words, "We have too much invested to quit."

See Also Cognitive Dissonance • Cost-Benefit • Framing

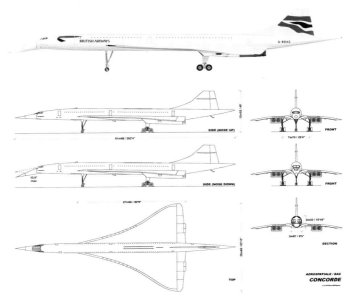

The British and French governments funded development of the Concorde SST long after they knew it would be an economic failure. Why? They had invested too much to quit.

133

Supernormal Stimulus

An exaggerated imitation that elicits a stronger response than the real thing.

- A supernormal stimulus is a variation of a familiar stimulus that elicits a response stronger than the stimulus for which it evolved.

- For example, female cuckoos sneak into the nests of other birds to lay their eggs. Because the cuckoo egg is typically larger and brighter than other eggs, the nest's owner gives it preferential attention. The size and brightness of the egg are supernormal stimuli to the unwitting adoptive mother.

- Supernormal stimuli dramatically influence the way people respond to brands, products, and services.

- Consider supernormal stimuli to increase attention and interest in logos, brands, products, and advertising. Explore stimuli involved in well-established biases and preferences for greatest effect.

See Also Baby-Face Bias • Gloss Bias • Waist-to-Hip Ratio

Exaggerations of things we have evolved to like—e.g., attractive features, fat and sugar, baby-faces—grab our attention.

134

Symmetry

A property of visual equivalence among elements.

- Symmetry is the most basic and enduring aspect of beauty. It is ubiquitous in nature.

- There are three basic types of symmetry: reflection, rotation, and translation.

- Reflection symmetry refers to mirroring elements around a central axis or mirror line.

- Rotation symmetry refers to rotating elements around a common center.

- Translation symmetry refers to locating equivalent elements in different areas of space.

- Use symmetry to convey balance, harmony, and stability. Use simple symmetries when recognition and recall are important. Use combinations of symmetries when aesthetics and interestingness are important.

See Also   Area Alignment • MAFA • Self-Similarity • Wabi-Sabi

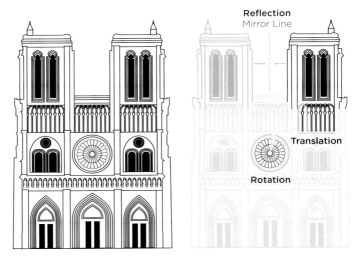

Reflection
Mirror Line

Translation

Rotation

The Notre Dame Cathedral uses multiple, complex symmetries to create a structure that is as beautiful as it is memorable.

135

Threat Detection

Threatening things are detected more efficiently than nonthreatening things.

- People reflexively detect and pay attention to certain threatening stimuli, such as spiders, snakes, predators, and angry human faces.

- This threat-detection ability provided early human ancestors with an adaptive advantage. Modern humans have inherited this ability.

- Things possessing key features of threatening stimuli can also trigger threat detection; for example, a wavy line that looks snakelike.

- Consider using key features of threatening stimuli in your designs to capture and hold attention.

See Also   Archetypes • Black Effects • Contour Bias
Freeze-Flight-Fight-Forfeit • Savanna Preference

In visually complex environments, threatening stimuli are detected more quickly than nonthreatening stimuli.

136

Top-Down Lighting Bias

A tendency to interpret objects as being lit from a single light source from above.

- People interpret dark areas of objects as shadows resulting from a light source above the object.

- Things that are lit from the top tend to look natural; whereas things that are lit from the bottom tend to look unnatural.

- Objects that are lighter at the top and darker at the bottom are interpreted to be convex, and objects that are darker at the top and lighter at the bottom are interpreted to be concave.

- Use a single top-left light source to depict natural-looking things. Explore bottom-up lighting when depicting unnatural-looking or foreboding things. Adjust the difference between light and dark areas to vary the perception of depth.

See Also 3D Projection • Figure-Ground Relationship
Threat Detection • Uncanny Valley

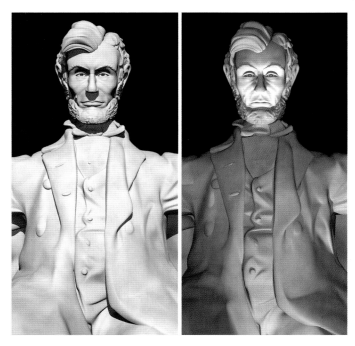

The Lincoln Memorial is usually lit top-down (left), but it has on occasion been lit bottom-up (right), revealing zombie Lincoln.

137

Uncanny Valley

Both abstract and realistic depictions of human faces are appealing, but faces in between are not.

- When a face is very close but not identical to a healthy human—as with mannequins or computer-generated renderings of people—it is considered repulsive. This is the uncanny valley.

- The uncanny valley refers to human features generally, but uncanny faces are the key source of the revulsion.

- The response is likely due to evolved mechanisms for detecting and avoiding people who are sick or dead.

- Until robots, computer renderings, and mannequins are indistinguishable from humans, favor more abstract versus realistic depictions of faces. Negative reaction is more sensitive to motion than appearance, so be particularly cognizant of jerky or unnatural facial expressions and eye movements.

See Also   Anthropomorphism • Attractiveness Bias
Threat Detection • Top-Down Lighting Bias

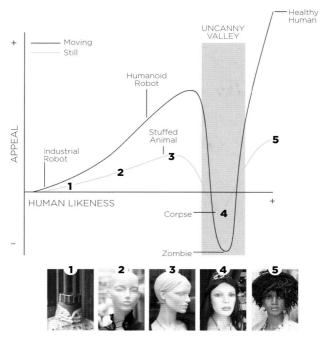

Mannequins that are realistic—but not perfectly realistic—are considered repulsive, dwelling in the uncanny valley.

138

Uncertainty Principle

Measuring things can change them, often making the results and subsequent measurements invalid.

• Measuring sensitive variables in a system can alter them, undermining the validity of the results and the instrument of measure.

• For example, event logging in computers increases the visibility of how the computer is performing, but it also consumes computing resources, which interferes with the performance being measured.

• The uncertainty introduced by a measure is a function of the sensitivity of variables in a system and the invasiveness of the measure. Beware using invasive measures, for they can permanently alter system behaviors and lead to unintended consequences.

• Use minimally invasive measures of performance whenever possible. Remember the maxim: Not everything that can be counted counts, and not everything that counts can be counted.

See Also   Abbe • Feedback Loop • Garbage In-Garbage out

March 21

9am
1/2 Cup Oatmeal
1/2 Cup Almond Milk
Handful Blueberries
1 Banana
Hot Tea with Lemon

1 pm
Can of Coke
2 Slices of Cheese Pizza

3pm
Chocolate Chip Cookie
Coffee with Sugar

6pm
1 Cup Brown Rice
1 Cup Black Beans
Salsa
2 Corn Tortillas

Many weight-loss programs promote keeping a food journal to lose weight—i.e., writing down everything you eat. Why does this work? Tracking what you eat changes how you eat.

139

Uniform Connectedness

Things connected by lines or boxes are perceived to be more related than things not connected.

- One of the Gestalt principles of perception.
- There are two strategies for applying uniform connectedness: connecting lines and common regions.
- Connecting lines touch two or more elements.
- Common regions enclose two or more elements with boxes or shaded areas.
- Uniform connectedness is the strongest grouping principle, and will overpower other grouping effects.
- Consider this principle to correct poorly grouped control and display configurations. Use common regions to group text and clusters of control elements. Use connecting lines to group individual elements and imply sequence.

See Also   Closure • Common Fate • Figure-Ground
Good Continuation • Proximity • Similarity

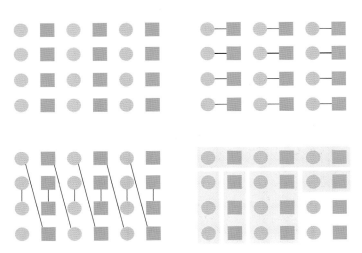

Uniform connectedness is a means of grouping elements and overriding competing cues like proximity and similarity.

140

Veblen Effect

A tendency to find a product more desirable because it has a high price.

- Proposed by the economist Thorstein Veblen.

- In certain cases, higher prices increase demand, and lower prices decrease demand.

- For example, the effect is most pronounced for items and services that signal status, such as art, jewelry, clothes, cars, fine wines, hotels, and luxury cruises.

- High prices increase perceived quality, and low prices decrease perceived quality.

- Consider the Veblen effect in marketing and pricing. Promote associations with high status people (e.g., celebrities). Employ strategies to discourage knockoffs, including legal protection, watermarking, and aggressive counter-advertising. Set prices high based on the intangible aspects of the offering.

See Also Classical Conditioning • Cognitive Dissonance
IKEA Effect • Left-Digit Effect • Scarcity

Electric cars are historically slow, ugly, and uncool. How to change this perception? Introduce a sexy electric car in limited numbers, associate it with people of status, and charge a premium. Once product perception makes the transformation from white elephant to white tiger, introduce lower-priced models. The Tesla Roadster: Veblen good.

141

Visibility

Things in clear view are more likely to be used than things not in clear view.

- Visible controls and information act as cues for what is and is not possible. Things that are not seen are less likely to be considered, and this is especially true when people are under stress.

- Accordingly, systems should clearly indicate their status, the key actions that can be performed, and the consequences of those actions once performed.

- Visibility increases probability of use when the number of options is small, but can overwhelm when the options are numerous. Beware kitchen-sink visibility.

- Design systems that clearly indicate their status, possible actions, and consequences of those actions. Balance visibility and complexity by selectively revealing and concealing controls and information based on context, relevance, and frequency of use.

See Also   Affordance • Control • Performance Load
Progressive Disclosure • Recognition Over Recall

Analysis of the Three Mile Island accident in 1979 revealed blind spots that made solving the problems almost impossible. In addition, alarms were blaring, lights were flashing, and critical system feedback was routed to a printer that could only print fifteen lines per minute—system status information was more than an hour behind for much of the crisis.

142

Visuospatial Resonance

A phenomenon in which different images are visible at different distances.

- Images rendered at a high spatial frequency appear as sharp outlines with little between-edge detail. High-spatial-frequency images are easily interpreted up close, but are not visible from a distance.

- Images rendered at a low spatial frequency appear as blurry images with little edge detail. Low-spatial-frequency images are not visible up close, but are easily interpreted from a distance.

- When images rendered at different spatial frequencies are combined, the result is visuospatial resonance. The effect can be stunning.

- Consider visuospatial resonance as a means of increasing the interestingness of posters and billboards, and masking sensitive information.

See Also Figure-Ground Relationship • Law of Prägnanz

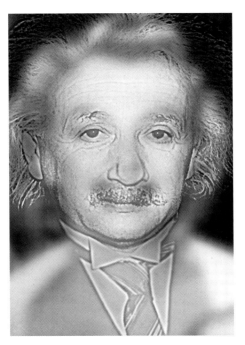

A hybrid image of two people at different spatial frequencies.
Up close: Albert Einstein. Far away: Marilyn Monroe.

von Restorff Effect

Uncommon things are easier to recall than common things.

- Proposed by German psychiatrist Hedwig von Restorff.

- The von Restorff effect results from the increased attention given to novel things relative to other things.

- For example, in the set of characters EZQL4PMBI, people will have heightened recall for the 4 because it is the only number in the sequence.

- The strength of the effect is a function of the novelty of the thing to be recalled.

- Apply the von Restorff effect to attract attention and increase memorability. Since recall for the middle items in a sequence is weaker than items at the beginning or end, use the von Restorff effect to boost recall for middle items. Consider unusual words, sentence constructions, and images to improve interestingness and recall.

See Also   Highlighting • Layering • Mnemonic Device
Serial Position Effects • Stickiness • Threat Detection

The highly distinctive form of the Wienermobile makes it—and the Oscar Mayer brand—completely unforgettable.

144

Wabi-Sabi

An aesthetic style that embodies naturalness, simplicity, and subtle imperfection.

• In sixteenth-century Japan, a student was tasked to tend the garden. He cleared the garden of debris and raked the grounds. Once the garden was perfectly groomed, he proceeded to shake a cherry tree, causing a few flowers and leaves to fall randomly to the ground. This is wabi-sabi.

• Wabi refers to beauty achieved through subtle imperfection. Sabi refers to beauty that comes with the passage of time.

• Wabi-sabi runs contrary to many innate biases and aesthetic conventions (e.g., preference for symmetry).

• Consider wabi-sabi when designing for audiences with sophisticated design sensibilities. Use elements that embody impermanence, imperfection, and incompleteness. Favor colors drawn from nature, natural materials and finishes, and organic forms.

See Also Desire Line • Ockham's Razor • Zeigarnik Effect

Deborah Butterfield uses found pieces of metal and wood in her horse sculptures. Equine wabi-sabi.

145

Waist-to-Hip Ratio

A preference for a particular ratio of waist size to hip size in men and women.

- The waist-to-hip ratio (WHR) is a significant factor in determining the attractiveness of people and anthropomorphic objects.

- WHR is primarily a function of testosterone and estrogen levels, and therefore serves as a biological signal of reproductive potential.

- WHR is calculated by dividing the circumference of the waist by the circumference of the hips.

- Men prefer women with a WHR between 0.67–0.80. Women prefer men with a WHR between 0.85–0.95.

- Consider WHR when depicting attractive people and anthropomorphic objects. Feminize objects by making their WHRs approximate 0.7 and masculinize objects by making their WHRs approximate 0.9.

See Also Anthropomorphism • Attractiveness Bias
Baby-Face Bias • Supernormal Stimulus

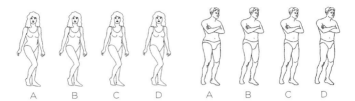

When asked to pick the most attractive bodies, people favored female A and male C, corresponding to WHRs of 0.70 and .90.

Mannequins have changed with the times, but their WHRs have been 0.70 for women and 0.90 for men for over five decades.

146

Wayfinding

The process of using spatial and environmental information to navigate to a destination.

- Wayfinding involves orientation, route decision, route monitoring, and destination recognition.

- Support orientation using clearly identifiable "you are here" landmarks and signs.

- Support route decisions by minimizing the number of navigational choices, and providing signs or prompts at key decision points.

- Support route monitoring by connecting locations with paths that have clear beginnings, middles, and ends. Provide regular confirmations that the path is leading to the destination.

- Support destination recognition by disrupting the flow of movement through a space using barriers or dead ends, and giving destinations clear identities.

See Also Mental Model • Progressive Disclosure
Rosetta Stone • Visibility

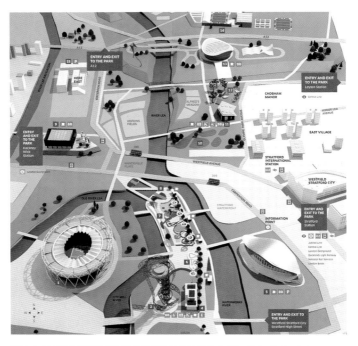

The London 2012 Olympic Park used landmarks, signage, simple routes, and destination markers to support wayfinding.

147

Weakest Link

An element designed to fail in order to protect more important elements from harm.

- Weakest links work in two ways: halting systems when they fail (e.g., electrical fuse), or activating mitigation systems when they fail (e.g., fire suppression system).

- Properly designed, the weakest link in a chain is the most important link.

- Weakest links predictably and reliably fail first.

- Weakest links are applicable to systems with cascading fault conditions—i.e., when there is a chain of events that can be interrupted.

- Consider adding weakest links to systems where failures occur as cascading events. Test and verify that weakest links only fail under the appropriate, predefined failure conditions.

See Also   Errors • Factor of Safety • Feedback Loop
Modularity • Redundancy

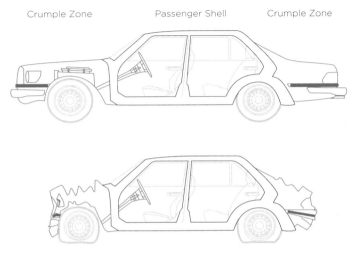

Crumple Zone   Passenger Shell   Crumple Zone

Crumple zones are one of the most significant automobile safety innovations of the twentieth century. The front and rear sections of vehicles are designed to crumple in a collision, reducing the energy transferred to the passenger shell.

148

White Effects

A set of cognitive and behavioral effects triggered by exposure to the color white.

- White is universally associated with goodness and security, likely due to an evolved association with daytime and a reduced vulnerability to predators.

- White signals passivity, submission, and cleanliness.

- Sports teams wearing predominately white uniforms are perceived to be less aggressive and less likely to cheat than those wearing dark colors. Accordingly, they incur fewer penalties.

- White products are generally perceived to be classy, high value, and timeless.

- Use white to increase perceived value in products, and perceived authority in people. Consider white to create a sense of peacefulness and submission.

See Also   Archetypes • Black Effects • Red Effects
Supernormal Stimulus • Threat Detection

Archetypal heroes wear mostly white to signal their goodness,
but with a dash of black to make them tough and intimidating.

149

Yellow Effects

A set of cognitive and behavioral effects triggered by exposure to the color yellow.

- Yellow is the most visible color to the eye, likely the result of an evolved sensitivity for detecting ripe fruit.

- When people eat a diet rich in fruits and vegetables, carotenoids give their skin a subtle, but detectable, yellow glow. This glow increases attractiveness.

- Yellow pills and chemicals are perceived to be stimulative and energetic.

- Yellow legal pads and yellow stickies may foster concentration and problem solving.

- Yellow clothes decrease attractiveness in both males and females more than any other color.

- Use yellow to grab attention, signal energy and potency, and promote problem solving. When attractiveness is key, generally avoid yellow apparel.

See Also   Green Effects • Supernormal Stimulus • White Effects

Painting fire trucks yellow versus red reduces the risk of visibility-related accidents by three times.

150

Zeigarnik Effect

A tendency to experience intrusive thoughts about a task that was interrupted or left incomplete.

- Proposed by Soviet psychiatrist and psychologist Bluma Zeigarnik.

- The unconscious mind seeks closure and completion, and preoccupies the conscious mind until it gets it. Accordingly, interrupted or incomplete tasks are better remembered than completed tasks.

- Once an interrupted task is completed, the recall benefits are lost. For example, waiters have better recall for in-process orders than served orders.

- The effect is strongest when people are highly motivated to complete a task.

- Apply the Zeigarnik effect to engage and maintain attention. For example, the "To be continued…" device is used in cliffhangers to keep people interested. Most importantly, never use the Zeigarnik effect to…

See Also   Closure • Flow • Gamification • IKEA Effect

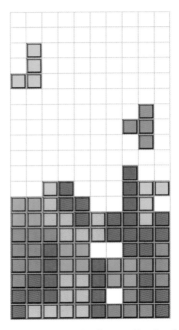

A never-ending series of puzzles leaves Tetris players shifting
blocks in their dreams, a condition dubbed the Tetris Effect.

Credits

3D Projection
Photograph by Flickr user Bill Hunt via Flickr through Creative Commons license.

Accessibility
Photograph by Gerry Manacsa.

Aesthetic-Usability Effect
Photograph courtesy of Arnell.

Archetypes
Images courtesy of Sue Weidemann Brill. Design concepts by Michael Brill, illustrations by Safdar Abidi. For more information about Michael Brill's work, please visit www.bosti.com.

Area Alignment
Images © 2008 Jupiterimages Corporation.

Attractiveness Bias
Photographs of Kennedy and Nixon © Bettman/Corbis.

Back-of-the-Dresser
Photographs by Paul Brennan/Hemera/Thinkstock

Biophilia Effect
Photograph by Urban Land Institute via Flickr through Creative Commons license.

Black Effects
"I Am Alex" photo by Robyn Arouty. For more information about Robyn's work, please visit www.robynarouty.com

Blue Effects
Images created by kovacevicmiro/iStock/Thinkstock.

Chunking
The Mona Lisa photomosaic is by Robert Silvers/Runaway Technology Inc. For more information about the work of Robert Silvers, please visit www.photomosiac.com. The Acacia Tree photograph is courtesy of U.S. Fish and Wildlife Service. The aqueduct photograph is by Prioryman via Wikipedia through Creative Commons license.

Classical Conditioning
Poster courtesy of Texas Department of Transportation. Photograph by Rob Buck. Advertising campaign by Sherry Matthews Advocacy Marketing. For more information about Jacqueline's story and recovery progress, please visit www.helpjacqui.com.

Credits, continued

Photograph of lips by dmitry zubarev/iStock/Thinkstock.

Golden Ratio
The Apple iPod is a registered trademark of Apple Computer, Inc.

Hierarchy of Needs
Photograph of the dog by Flickr user Richard Masoner/Cyclelicious. Photograph of paintball helmet by Flickr user Gordon Tarpley. Photograph of drone by Flickr user Don McCullough. Photograph of *PBS NewsHour* helmet by *PBS NewsHour*. All photographs via Flickr through Creative Commons license.

Hunter-Nurturer Bias
Reprinted from *Evolution and Human Behavior*, Vol. 23(6), Gerianne M. Alexander and Melissa Hines, "Sex differences in response to children's toys in non-human primates (Cercopithecus aethiops sabaeus)", pp. 467-479, Copyright 2002, with permission from Elsevier.

IKEA Effect
Photograph by monkeybusinessimages/iStock/Thinkstock.

Iteration
Photograph courtesy of NASA.

Mere-Exposure Effect
Posters courtesy of Ota Nepily, Studio Gappo, Brno, Czech Republic. The posters on this page and similar works are available for purchase at www.poster.wz.cz. Special thanks to Petr Kuca for his assistance.

Modularity
Photograph courtesy of NewDealDesign, LLC. Photography by Mark Serr Photography.

Nudge
Photograph by Paul Downey via Flickr through Creative Commons license.

Ockham's Razor
The Apple iMac is a registered trademark of Apple Computer, Inc.

Credits, continued

Storytelling
Photographs of Civil Rights Memorial courtesy of Southern Poverty Law Center. Photographs by John O'Hagan. Designed by Maya Lin.

Structural Forms
Photographs of RDFW courtesy of Geocell Systems. Pod photograph courtesy of Sanford Ponder, Icosa Village, Inc.

Sunk Cost Effect
Profile drawing by Emoscopes via Wikipedia through GNU Free Documentation License. Schmematics by Julien.scavini via Wikipedia through Creative Commons Attribution-Share Alike 3.0 Unported license.

Supernormal Stimulus
Image of Superhero by Gazometr/iStock/Thinkstock. Photograph of Cheesecake by Lesyy/iStock/Thinkstock. Image of Po © 1996-2003 Ragdoll Ltd. Used with permission. All rights reserved.

Threat Detection
Photograph of spider by GlobalP/iStock/Thinkstock.

Top-Down Lighting Bias
3D Model by Dan Deentremont from TurboSquid.

Uncanny Valley
Photograph of mannequin one © 2008 Jupiterimages Corporation. Photograph of mannequin two by Flickr user Dierk Schaefer via Flickr through creative commons license. Photograph of mannequin three by Flickr user Jesse Swallow via Flickr through Creative Commons license.

Veblen Effect
Photograph of Tesla Roadster courtesy of Tesla Motors, Inc.

Visibility
Photograph courtesy of United States Department of Energy

Visuospatial Resonance
Hybrid image of Einstein and Monroe courtesy of Aude Olivia, MIT. Source images for Einstein © Bettman/Corbis and Monroe, Getty Images/Hulton Archive. Special thanks to Aude Oliva.

von Restorff Effect
Photograph by Jonathunder via Wikipedia through GNU Free Documentation License.

Acknowledgments

The authors would like to thank the many contributors whose works are featured, and ask that readers review the Credits section to learn more about these very talented individuals and companies. We would also like to extend a special thanks to Scott O'Connor for his modeling and graphic design support.